DANGEROUS DRIVING

DANGEROUS DRIVING

– A life behind the wheel –

Bill Reynolds

Seeker
Publishing & Distribution
in the Channel Islands

Published in 2015 by
Seeker Publishing
Units 1 & 2 Elms Farm
La Mare Vineyards
La Route de la Hougue Mauger
St Mary
Jersey
JE3 3BA

www.seekerpublishing.com

Origination by Seaflower Books
www.ex-librisbooks.co.uk

Printed and bound by CPI Group (UK) Ltd, Croydon, CR0 4YY

ISBN 978-0-9932657-5-4

*This book is dedicated to my wife Doreen,
my children Christopher, Jacquie & Nicola, and
my grandchildren Sophie, Vanessa,
Lawrence, Edward, Henry & Jack.*

CONTENTS

Foreword

During my time as Bailiff, my wife and I had the privilege of getting to know a number of Jersey's Normandy veterans. Bill Reynolds is one of those veterans. I am delighted he has decided, with the help of Chris Stone, to tell his story and I am honoured to have been asked to write a foreword.

The book starts with Bill's childhood in Jersey. It is clear that, even then, he was not someone who would ever shirk a dare or a challenge! In 1940, when he was 16, his mother – his father had died when he was nine – faced the agonising dilemma faced by so many Jersey people as Hitler's troops advanced across France. Should the family stay or should they evacuate to the UK? She chose to evacuate with Bill, but one of his brothers remained in the Island. Bill then experienced the full horror of the Blitz and writes movingly of those times. Once he was old enough he enlisted and in due course joined the Royal Army Service Corps, Guards Armoured Division. Following the Normandy landings he participated in the push across Europe, telling of his experiences in the battle for Caen, the liberation of Brussels, Arnhem, the Battle of the Bulge and other significant events.

Bill is a superb raconteur and he gives a vivid account of what it was like to be part of these terrible events. What shines through very strongly is his zest for life, his courage and his modesty, as well as his humour. And that has not diminished with age! Bill and his fellow veteran Harry Fenn represented Jersey's veterans at the ceremonies on 6 June 2014 to mark the 70th anniversary of the Normandy landings. It was a very long day, beginning in the early hours of the morning with a drive from the hotel in

Avranches and followed by events at Bayeux, Arromanches and Caen. By the end of the day, most of us were beginning to flag, but Bill and Harry were still going strong. It is perhaps not surprising therefore that, although he is now in his 90s, Bill says in the book that he often complains about other people driving their cars too slowly and getting in his way!

This book brings out the courage and fortitude of those who risked their lives to secure our liberty in the Second World War. Once I started it I could not put it down and I thoroughly commend it as an informative, interesting and at times humorous account of one soldier's experience of the war.

Sir Michael Birt

Introduction

'I used to race over there,' says Bill as we drive in the sunshine past the Five Mile Road. It's a misleading name; the main part of the road is only about three and a half miles long. But it goes flat and reasonably straight right next to the beach on the west coast of Jersey. Sand dunes climb up from the sea grass beside it, and golden sand stretches away from the shore. When the tide is out, it leaves acres of firm, flat beach. They still hold races there, with people hammering souped-up bangers around orange cones to mark out a course. Modest crowds come to watch if the weather is good.

But it's a far cry from the glory days of sand racing in Jersey, just after the war. A time when men like Bill would take cars which would now be worth hundreds of thousands of pounds, strip them down to the bare essentials, then see just how fast they could go in front of thousands of spectators. Health and Safety was a long way in the future, and they used a potent mix of benzine and ethanol to power their cars faster and faster. Their only protection was an old pair of flying overalls and some youthful exuberance.

Driving cars, especially on beaches, is in Bill's blood. He started at less than ten years old, driving Model T vans loaded with ice cream. A little more than ten years later he was driving onto the invasion beaches of Normandy in a waterproofed truck, before fighting his way across France. Along the way he trained on, borrowed, or stole, all sorts of other vehicles. From Jeeps to DUKWs, ammo trucks to Sherman tanks, German staff cars to motorbikes, he drove them all.

So it's no surprise that after the war he became a very successful motor racer, not just on the beach but on sprints and hill climbs too. Motor racing became his life, his escape from the war and its memories. It did its best to kill him, but that didn't put him off.

This is the story of a man, now into his nineties, who still loves to get behind the wheel.

He is amazingly sprightly for a man of his age. At veterans ceremonies he still marches if there is a band. He stands during the long service, proud in his beret and medals, and is always ready to talk to inquisitive youngsters afterwards.

It wasn't always like that though. In common with many veterans, after the war he tried to wipe all the unpleasant memories from his mind. No one asked him about what he had done. He told no one, not even his closest family and friends. It wasn't until fifty years after it all finished that he realised that people might be interested, and joined the newly formed Normandy Veterans Association. He had to send away for the medals he deserved but had never been awarded.

I am of a generation which owes a huge debt of gratitude to Bill and his comrades, many of whom didn't come back. They experienced things which would be enough to make cowards of us all, but they kept calm and carried on, because they knew it was right. Theirs was a generation which did its duty. They saw their friends die, and destruction on an epic scale. It's no wonder he didn't want to talk about it for so long; we are very lucky that now Bill and many other men and women who lived through those dark times are finally ready to tell their story.

Of course, listening to Bill, the memories weren't all dark; he remembers some very funny stories too with a twinkle in his eye and a mischievous sense of humour, often at his own expense. It's always struck me how many veterans look back on their time in the army with a sense of enjoyment, despite the horrors they had to endure.

We wrote this book together at the house he still shares with his wife

Doreen. A word about this marvellous lady, whose age I won't disclose, but is similar to Bill's. Often when I turned up at the house, rain or shine, she would be out and about gardening. On one occasion she was wielding a pitchfork and digging up a big rock which was spoiling her flower beds. Somehow she managed it while still looking effortlessly elegant. With sparkling blue eyes and a great sense of fun, she kept us supplied with tea and biscuits, and I am grateful to her for her smiles, encouragement and support.

It has been a pleasure and privilege to work with Bill; no question I asked was too much, even if it touched on painful memories. He relived emotions which had been buried for years, and was happy to share them with me even when they were difficult. His generosity always took me aback; he always made sure he had my favourite Bourbon biscuits in the tin, and the kettle went on as soon as I arrived. It was rare that I left empty-handed too, and I regularly went home with a bottle of wine or a bag of fruit grown in his garden.

Bill Reynolds is someone who can tell us of extraordinary times gone by – Covent Garden as a bustling fruit market, the stark reality of bombed-out London, the ferocity of the fight to take Caen, the danger of driving across Nijmegen Bridge under fire, and the desperation of the Battle of the Bulge. For most of us just names in history books; talking to Bill they become alive and very real.

But our conversations were often dominated by extraordinary cars. From souped-up, high-octane racing cars to majestic tourers, he has driven and loved them all.

I had a perfect view out over Five Mile Road that sunny day. I was sitting in the back of a convertible 1932 two and a half litre Lagonda which Bill keeps in his garage. It is spotless. It makes a wonderful noise. It stops traffic. And Bill was driving. Of course.

Chris Stone

Chapter 1

THE KING OF THE KIDS

Walworth Road in London was a busy place in the twenties. The electric tram had recently been installed, to take workmen home and help people get to the shops. The Elephant and Castle Cinematograph had opened just a few years before, so people could enjoy all the latest films. There were toy shops, butchers and bakers, theatres; it was a really busy, bustling place. And it got busier on 22 June, 1923, when I was born.

My dad had a fruit and veg shop, and we all lived above it. My earliest memory is of being in my pram at the back of the shop, in the yard where the stables were. It was all covered in straw. I saw a great big rat running across the yard, which was quite frightening for me as a baby! Dad never had a motor vehicle to do all of his deliveries. He used a horse and cart to do his rounds. My brothers used to tell me how they would have to get up at four in the morning and take the cart down to Covent Garden, which of course used to be a fruit and vegetable market. They would fill the cart for about ten shillings, then bring it all back to the shop to sell. The whole family used to help out. My sister Nellie was the eldest, she was about thirteen when I was born. My brother George was twelve, Sid was eleven, Charlie was eight and Violet was three. They had grown up during the Great War, and Mum used to say that she could go down to the local market and buy dinner for the whole family for sixpence! Dad had been in the army, but he never spoke to me much about it. I know he had been gassed, but he died when I was still young.

It hadn't been easy for him and Mum. Mum's grandfather, Mr MacMillan, had been a very rich man. He had properties on Oxford Street, and was from high society. Eventually he dropped the Mac from his name, so Mum's maiden name was Millan. But when he died, his son – Mum's father – wouldn't claim the money. He said his parents had never wanted him, so he didn't want their money. It all went to the Crown. Mum used to say that the family and its descendants should never have worked, there was so much money. I never met them, only my dad's mother. We used to visit her, but she was very old and I was very young so I don't remember much about her. Mum told me later that one of her brothers had been killed during the war, and another had gone down with the Titanic.

We used to be able to play in the street – although there were trams, there wasn't much other traffic because not many people had cars in those days. I can remember playing with a ball which rolled beneath a great big truck which was driven by chains, a great big noisy thing. I remember the fear of crawling underneath that truck, between those big chains, but I wanted to get my ball back!

It wasn't long though before we were on the move. Mum and Dad went away on a holiday to Jersey and fell in love with the place. While they were there they saw a business for sale, on the corner of Market Street and Halkett Street. It was an off-licence and grocery shop. They decided there and then to buy it. They came back to London, packed us all up, and we were off to Jersey!

What a contrast that was. London was full of noise and people and enormous buildings. The clanking of the trams, the shouting of market traders, people in a hurry on the Underground. Jersey is such a tiny place in comparison! Nine miles by five, and right next to France; you can see it from the east coast of the island really clearly. And it was nearly all countryside. Potato farming was the main thing then, and tomatoes too. It was far more quiet and peaceful than London. We went to live in the capital, St Helier, because that's where Dad wanted to set up business.

My earliest memory of the island is walking up New Street with my

Mum and Dad

Myself as a boy

sister because we were farmed out to a Mrs Grey who lived in Dumaresq Street. This was while Mum and Dad sorted out the shop and the living space for us there. I remember hiding under the kitchen table while this lady banged the top of it with a cane. I must have been a naughty boy!

But eventually they sorted out the flat above the shop, and that's where we all went to live. I remember playing outside when Dad turned up with a bull-nosed Morris car which he drove up onto the pavement before going into the shop. It was his first vehicle, but it looked like a boat! So we all jumped in it and started playing, pretending it actually was a boat, and I tied it up to the drainpipe like a boat to a harbour. When Dad came out it wouldn't start, so I got a bit of a smack! And that was my first experience of being in a car. It was very exciting for us. Soon he got some Model T vans as well. He had an ice cream factory in Columbus Street, and during the summer he and my brothers would go around the beaches selling ice cream from them. It began when he used to go to the ex-servicemen's club in Queen Street, and Jocelyn the butcher said he'd bought four Model T vans, which was one too many. My old man said, 'Well, I could do with an extra one,' so they played a game of crib for the spare van and Dad won it! So there he was driving around selling ice creams from a van which said 'Jocelyn the Butcher. Pleased to Meet You, Meat to Please You.' written down the side of it!

When I was old enough I used to go out selling with them, although it was always my brothers who actually drove the vans. There were other blokes who used to go around town with these tricycles selling ice cream too. It was all held in metal containers inside wooden containers to try to keep it cold while it was taken around. The space between the containers was packed with ice. I think we'd moved to Journeaux Street by then, and at the end of the day the tricycles and vans would come back to us, and there would usually be some ice creams left. Of course in those days there was no way to preserve them, they had to be used the same day. So I became the King of the Kids, because all the kids in the neighbourhood used to come round to have a taste. If I didn't like them they didn't get one! I remember it being really good ice cream too. Dad used to make it using the best, full cream Jersey milk. He was in competition with Smith and Sons in Cannon Street, which was just around the corner. I never got tired of the taste of it. We used to go to the most popular beaches to sell it, and I would help my brothers. You'd have a wafer which was held in this little gadget. Then you'd get a scoop of the ice cream and put it on the wafer, then another wafer on the top to make an ice cream sandwich.

During the winter we sold crisps around the pubs. Dad would make them, just like Smith's Crisps, and there were twelve packets to a tin. The factory was just next to the off-licence in Aquila Road, by the ice cream factory. Next door was a fish and chip shop. I used to come home after school and work on the slicing machine, which cut up the potatoes to make the crisps. They went into a deep pan to be fried, then they were weighed out and put into bags with a little roll of salt. You could choose how much salt you wanted when you ate them. Once they were ready you could pack them into boxes and load them into a van to take them round the pubs. And not just in St Helier, we used to take them all over the island. One place I used to look forward to visiting was La Pulente, the pub at the end of the Five Mile Road, right next to the sea on the west coast. Every time we went there the landlord would give me a cassis to drink! I think he was Percy Kemp, the father of Clive Kemp, whom I met years later as a Normandy veteran.

It was going on these trips, selling goods around the island, that gave me my interest for cars. Right from my earliest years, as soon as I could reach the pedals, I was driving them. They were easy in those days. By the time I was fourteen, I would drive while my brother sat and discussed business with his partner George. That was after the time of the Model T vans though; they were quite difficult because you had to start them using a big starter handle. Once my brother was trying to crank it over and it kicked back and broke his arm. When he had his arm in plaster the old man said, 'Come on, you don't need two arms to do this work, get on with it!'

Often on a Sunday we'd all go out for a long drive in Dad's maroon touring car. We'd go to places like Greve de Lecq and St Aubin's village where the parish hall is now. It was the Terminus Hotel. I can remember we paid five shillings for a lobster tea.

They were lovely parents to me. I remember when my sister and I were still very young we'd burst into their bedroom early on Sunday mornings and dance about. My sister danced like a fairy, and I danced like a horse! Dad always used to say, 'Willie's won! He's the best dancer!' and he'd give me a thruppeny bit. He always used to keep them for me and give me half a dozen. I had a bike when I was about seven years old, much to the envy of the other kids who didn't have one. Most of the working people couldn't afford one, let alone a car. They were a bit envious. I remember cycling down Garden Lane and two thugs stopped me. They said, 'Come on, we want to ride your bike.' I said no, and one of them hit me with a bit of four by two wood, which cracked me just above my left eye. I've still got the scar.

Of course I couldn't play all the time – I was young and had to go to school. I started at Halkett Place School when I was five years old. I used to go there with my sister. But I was only there for a year before I moved to St Mark's. I liked school, and was always top of the class for arithmetic. Shortly before Dad died they put me down to go to Victoria College, and you had to be clever to get in there. But when Dad died we lost a lot of money, a lot of our things had to be sold off for very little, and Mum didn't have any income so I never went there. My brothers said they would pay for me but I said no.

It began with a fire. I was nine years old. A man had come into the shop in Aquila Road just before closing time. He dropped a cigarette behind the biscuit tins, which were always stacked in front of the counter. Nobody noticed, and we all went upstairs to bed. At about one o'clock in the morning the shop was well and truly blazing away; we woke up and I can remember the room being full of smoke. It was terrifying, and we had to get out quick. We all assembled outside, and the fire brigade came to try and put it out. Dad was helping to get the vehicles out from the yard at the back of the factory. He caught a cold, then flu. But he wanted to carry on working, so he asked the doctor if he could go out. The doctor said, 'Of course,' so he did. But then he caught pneumonia, then double pneumonia.

I went into the hospital to see him with Mum. There he was, sitting on his bed, counting out his small change. I can see him now, very clearly. In those days though, there wasn't really a cure for pneumonia, and he died. They put his coffin in the front room with the lid open; it was how things were done then. Every time I had to pass that room I used to run. I was terrified of it. I didn't go to the funeral, I was too young.

It was the end of our happy times in Aquila Road. We had to leave because Mum couldn't really afford to run the shop, the factory and the house. One of the problems was that Dad had bought a new Dodge van from a place called Stevenson's, and owed twenty-five pounds for fuel and maintenance there. When he died, Stevenson's just came and took the vehicle back to cover the debt. In those days they could do that. We had to sell the ice-cream tricycles, which had been bought for fifteen pounds, for just five shillings. We moved from Aquila Road to a place by the church on Great Union Road. Then there was another quick move to a place called Nelson House on Nelson Street. It was by the old fire station in St Helier.

My brothers managed to carry on our family business, getting hundredweight blocks of ice from the freezers in Waterworks Valley. By then, they had moved on to selling fish, and all three of them were working together. So they were out working, Mum was having to cope on her own, and I started getting into all kinds of scrapes.

Chapter 2

LUCKY ESCAPES

I was quite independent as a child, and was always having adventures. I'm quite lucky I lived to tell the tale though, after some of them!

When I was four they had recently built the bridge to the pool at Havre des Pas. It's a sea pool, close to the road to the east of St Helier. It was quite a popular place to go, because it had its own cafe, and places for people to sit down and enjoy themselves. The problem was, when the tide came in, the cafe and everything got cut off, so they built a bridge across to it from the road for people to walk on. Now to make the supports for the uprights they used old pieces of railway line, bent into shape and driven into the sand and rock. At the bottom of each support was a big concrete block, to make sure they were firmly anchored. Because they stuck out at an angle, and were curved, they were perfect as slides when the tide was out, and all the kids were going up onto the bridge and sliding down. Even my sister was doing it, so I thought, 'I'll try that!' Off I went – straight down, headfirst, into the concrete block! I can remember running home, pouring with blood, and crying my eyes out. It gave me a scar above my eye; the opposite side to where the thug hit me after nicking my bike years later! You can still see them both, even today.

When I was about seven I was at West Park swimming pool. It's a big horseshoe-shaped concrete pool on the beach just in front of St Helier, so it was really popular with everyone coming from town. It gets filled up as the tide comes in, then when it goes out the water is trapped inside. It means you can have a swim no matter what the tide is doing. We used to go to the beach whenever we had any spare time. I think I'd just about learned to swim by then.

On this particular day in summer we were playing on the wall of the pool as the tide was coming in over the hot sand. It was a beautiful day, and we were taking it in turns to dive into the sea, on the outside of the pool. Then one of my little friends said, 'I wonder if the sea's this warm in the pool?' And me being an idiot, I dived in. But it must have been a big spring tide because just as I did, a big wave came over the wall too. What I should have done was to swim with it, towards the shore. But I tried to go against it, back to the wall. I can remember swimming and swimming, against this wall of water, and getting weaker and weaker. More waves were crashing over me, and I was gasping and swallowing water, and starting to panic. It's true what they say, all of your life goes through your mind, your family, everything; and then suddenly everything was blank. Gone. I was out.

The next thing I remember I was lying on the beach with a man trying to pump the water out of my lungs. I had swallowed loads of water. He saved my life, but once I started to cough and splutter, and he could see I was going to be all right, he just stood up and walked away. I never told my parents, because I wanted to be allowed to keep going there to see my friends! In those days all the kids used to head down to West Park. It was much easier then, you didn't have all the cars and things to worry about.

My next adventure was when I was eight years old and my brothers and sisters decided to go for a swim at First Tower first thing in the morning, about seven a.m.! I ran down the beach. Suddenly I heard the roar of engines. I turned to the right and saw a Jersey airlines plane, a de Havilland Rapide, coming straight for me. The pilot spotted me and lifted the plane right over me. I froze with fear, but the plane went safely over my head. In those days Jersey didn't have a proper airport, and passenger planes used to land on the beach.

It wasn't long after that that I had another lucky escape. Alongside the shop in Aquila Road was a row of cottages. There was a big entrance there to get to them. And from there we used to have access to the big flat roof of the factory, with a ladder. I used to climb up there to have a look about, to see what was going on next door. One day I was up there on the roof when my mother called me inside for a meal. I can't remember what was so interesting to me, but I started walking backwards towards the ladder so I could keep watching. Now in the ceiling of the factory was a glass skylight, and because I wasn't looking where I was going I fell backwards through it! Back I went with a huge crash as the glass shattered, and I just plummeted towards the factory floor below. But typically for me, I was lucky; I landed on a big coiled hosepipe which cushioned the landing. It knocked the air out of me, but I wasn't badly hurt. Believe it or not, that hosepipe was right next to the ice breaking machine. That had a moving belt leading to these wheels with great big six inch spikes sticking out of them. You'd put the big blocks of ice on the belt and they would get smashed up by these whirling spikes. If I'd fallen just a foot or two to the left or right I wouldn't be here today, no question!

When I was eight, I went on a bike ride with my friends to St Brelade. That was a fair old ride, along the sea front about four or five miles from St Helier. It was a great thing to do. We went to a place just around the corner from St Brelade's Bay, and parked our bikes. There weren't any houses about, and not much of a path. We wanted to go to the beach, and we could see it a long way below us. We headed down this steep grassy slope towards it. It got steeper and steeper, and then suddenly I slipped, and was sliding down this grass verge, heading towards a thirty-foot drop with these huge boulders at the bottom; and over I went. I flew through the air, heading for the big piles of rocks on the beach. I landed with a thump. When I came to, my mates were telling me how lucky I had been, again. I'd landed upside down, with my head between two of the biggest rocks, so although I'd bruised my shoulders my head was all right! I managed to climb out despite the pain in my shoulders, then ride all the way home.

Despite that, I got quite fond of rock climbing. There used to be a quarry near the Portelet Hotel, on the cliffs not far from St Brelade, and we used to climb up the face that looked out to sea. It was quite dodgy, because the cliff was quite crumbly, with a lot of loose stone and gravel. Once I climbed up it, but only got about half way before I realised I was stuck, I couldn't go up or down. No matter how much I tried, there was nowhere else to put my hands or feet, in any direction. So I just had to stay there, hoping I didn't slip, yelling my head off in fright: 'Get somebody to help me!' My mates ran off, and after what seemed like ages and ages a man appeared at the top of the cliff. He lowered a rope down and dragged me up to safety.

I didn't learn my lesson though. Close by to that was a place where they used to dump unwanted stone over the cliff. They had a little wooden truck on wheels which ran on rails all the way down the slope to carry it. The rails stuck out over the edge. When the truck had flown down to the end of the rails, it would jerk to a stop, the bottom would automatically drop away, and the stone would fall. Of course we used to jump on and enjoy riding the truck down as far as we dared, just for devilment. It was really exciting, actually! I used to go with it all the way. When the bottom dropped out you'd hang on tight to the sides to stop yourself falling, then somehow pull the bottom back up. Then your mates could pull the truck back up to the top of the hill for another go. I can't remember anyone ever being there when we were playing, so if anyone had gone over the edge there wouldn't have been anybody to help.

Then there was the time my mate shot me. We were riding our bikes back from school, and we all had these five shilling Dyno airguns. They fired these darts that were attached to little feathers, or lead pellets. So there we were, riding along, when Graham Taylor turned around and shot me! Luckily it hit me on the lapel of my jacket where the cloth is quite thick, right above my heart! The thickness of the material stopped it from hurting me too much, thank goodness.

There was also my adventure with Nobby's skiff; that started a run of bad luck for me and boats. Nobby was this bloke who had a little business in St Helier harbour, renting out sailing dinghies and skiffs, small boats that you could row about on. We always fancied having a go. We used to play around the harbour after school and look at the boats. This one time, me and my mates managed to rake up sixpence between us. Nobby used to charge a shilling for an hour on one of these skiffs, going from the landing down where the Maritime Museum is now. We went to see him, ready to give him our sixpence for half an hour. But he wasn't there, so we thought we'd just take one and then give him the money when we got back. So we got into the skiff, pushed it into the harbour, and were rowing like mad, having a great time. The only problem was, our backs were facing the harbour entrance, and we didn't see the mail boat coming in. It was a great big ship, and we bashed straight into it. Our little skiff was only made of a few planks, and there was no way it could withstand that. It split into bits, and sank immediately, right in the middle of the harbour! The three of us were dumped right in the water, fully dressed, and had to swim like mad to get back to land. We came out at the steps by the yacht club, and shot off quick. Needless to say, we never went back to see Nobby, and he never got his sixpence!

I'd got the boating bug though, so I decided to build myself a canoe. I laid down a wooden keel and made some metal ribs to bolt to it. Then I covered the lot with canvas, and smothered that with boiled linseed oil to make it waterproof. Finally I painted it to make it look nice, because I was very proud of my efforts. I showed it to all my mates, and we decided we'd paddle it from West Park – where I'd nearly drowned before – to Elizabeth Castle, about a mile out in the bay. It was all fine for a while as we paddled away, with a nice smooth sea. But about half way out it started to get a bit choppy, and that's when we realised that my home-made canoe didn't have enough freeboard – in other words I hadn't made it deep enough! Sure enough, it started to fill with water very quickly and then *whoosh* – she sank right beneath us! Once again I was swimming about, fully dressed, trying to get to land because my boat had sunk.

As I climbed out dripping wet, I decided I'd have to buy a proper, new canoe. So I did. It cost me ten bob, and as soon as I got it my brother helped me out by taking it in the car down to the Old Harbour. The problem was, when we got there the tide was halfway out. Instead of waiting for higher water so I could launch it safely, I put it in the few inches that were in the harbour and jumped in. Off I went, rowing like mad across the harbour again. What I hadn't realised was that by jumping in, I'd squashed it against a bit of glass or a sharp stone on the bottom. So there was this little tear in the bottom of the canoe. Guess what happened when I was about halfway across?! You'd think I'd have learned my lesson, but it wasn't to be the last time a boat would sink under me in embarrassing circumstances – more of that later!

Another, more profitable adventure was when I was playing on Queen's Road one day, not far from our house. There was a man walking along near me, when all of a sudden I heard this tinkling sound; he'd dropped half a crown out of his pocket! So of course I ran along and picked it up; a moment later I heard the same sound. He'd dropped another one! So I had that one too; in fact I ended up with seven half crowns. By the time I had picked up the last one the man had disappeared, I don't know where he went, maybe into a pub. So I went home and said to Mum, 'Look what I've found!' But she said, 'You naughty boy, you should have given them back!' That was a lot of money in those days, when wages were about thirty shillings a week.

Among all these adventures I was still going to school, which I enjoyed, and helping out with the business at home. When I was thirteen though, my mum decided she wanted to go back to London for a while to be with her sisters. They were both working in the Royal Hotel in Marble Arch. She took me with her, and we lived there for about ten months in a place which I think was called Warner Street, just off the Old Kent Road. It was later destroyed in the Blitz. I had to say goodbye to the beaches and sunshine for a while, and get back to the noise and rush of London. What a difference! Jersey was all bright and clean, with ice cream and potato fields. London was all grimy and dirty, and there was no fresh air or swimming pools. But actually I didn't mind it. I went to school there, and quite enjoyed myself. I remember the craze at the time was skates, and every kid in the area was rolling about on them. I got some too, and used to whizz about with them. We had a lot of laughs at school. I remember there being an electrical point outside one of the doors. We used to put a wire in there, then about twelve or fourteen of us would hold hands and *brrzzzt!* we'd all get an electric shock. It wasn't my idea ... and of course I never learned my lesson, as you'll see.

On Saturdays when I wanted to go out, I used to raid my money box. I worked out how to tip it up and poke a knife into the slot so I could get a penny out of it. I can remember my mum really shouting at me because she found there was only about tuppence left in there when there should have been about two bob! A penny would get me down onto the Underground, and I'd spend all day travelling about on the trains, all over London, before I came back up on the same station. All on a penny ticket!

I'd go down to the Old Kent Docks too, and Tower Bridge, and really explore the sights of London. I went to the old Trocadero Cinema at the Elephant and Castle. Mum was working, so once I finished school I was free to wander off wherever I wanted to. I was quite an independent lad; I enjoyed wandering about on my own. But I still missed Jersey.

I was relieved when the time came to go back there. By the time I came back to the island I was fourteen, which was old enough to leave school, so I never went back. My brother George said I should learn a trade, so I would always be able to earn my living. In those days, all young people like me learned a trade, like plumbing or carpentry. You'd get two and six, or half a crown, a week. Maybe they thought I'd grow up a bit! That was in 1937. Jersey was still a peaceful place, just as we had left it. Nobody could have thought that war was just over the horizon, and that I wouldn't have long to enjoy the island before I had to leave again.

Chapter 3

A WORKING MAN

So there I was, back in Jersey with the sea and sunshine, only now I was fourteen and ready to go to work. I was living at home again, and wanted to earn a wage. My brothers helped out, and got me an apprenticeship as a plasterer and tiler. It wasn't easy though, and I had a lot to learn. In those days tiles were fastened onto the wall using cement, not adhesive like they use today. I had to learn quickly, because you were expected to be able to do a proper job; it wasn't like being at school. One of my first jobs was working on the Jersey Electricity building in Broad Street, in St Helier. We were installing a toilet. We'd finished all the tiling, and they left me to clean it all up, wiping down the waste cement and things. I was using a wet cloth, and everything around was wet too because we'd just finished off. To power the lights and tools and things they had electrical cables hanging from the ceiling, not attached to proper plugs like you would get today. To give me light I had one in the cubicle where I was working, with a light bulb in the end of it. I was nearly done when this bloke came over and asked me if he could use the cable. I said, 'Yes, I'm all but finished', and off he went. I stood up and unscrewed the light bulb so he could use the cable. But as I did that, somehow my fingers must have touched the contacts on the end of the lead. My hand was wet, and I was standing on a wet floor, and the next thing I knew I was being thrown around this toilet, smashing into the walls and everything. Tiles were falling off and smashing everywhere, and I was making a hell of a racket. The bloke who had asked me for the lead came running back, and had the presence of mind to pull it off my finger. He probably saved my life. I was dazed, I didn't know where I was, my finger was burning… It took me a long time to recover, but I didn't need to go to hospital. And of course, all the tiling needed to be re-done!

Another time I hurt my foot quite badly because a bloke let go of a scaffolding pole. We were in the back yard of the site, building a new part. He was holding this great big scaffolding pole upright, when he decided to let go of it. It fell over, and landed really hard right on my big toe. It hurt like hell, and I knew it was quite bad. Despite the pain in my foot, I jumped on my bike and pedalled over to the hospital as fast as I could.

When I got there the nursing sister managed to get my shoe off. Don't forget there weren't really many painkillers in those days, so she just got on with it. I was sitting in the chair in this room, and she looked at my foot and said 'Look out of the window.' So I did, and while I was looking out of the window I felt this ripping, and I jumped out of my skin; she'd pulled my toenail off with a pair of pliers! It must have been damaged when the pole fell on it, and she thought the best thing to do was to get rid of it. She bandaged it all up, covered in blood, and off I went. To this day, that nail doesn't grow straight.

While I was getting on with learning my trade, and trying not to be electrocuted or injured again, my three brothers were running a successful fish business. They had three vans, and used to go all round the island selling it to people, and hotels and restaurants. But by then people had started to become aware, even in little Jersey, that war was coming. Hitler was building up huge armies and wasn't just going to keep them for show, he was a real threat. So in 1938 and 1939, men started joining up, and my brother Charlie decided he would be one of them. That meant that one of the family fish vans didn't have a driver. To begin with they employed this chap, and I went with him to show him the round. But he wasn't very good as a salesman, and they got rid of him. So there was only one obvious choice; I threw in my apprenticeship, and joined my brothers' firm. That was in 1939, and I was sixteen. What a great job for me, driving for a living!

I had already learned to drive years before. My first experience had been when I was about five, sitting on my brother's lap, steering a Model T Ford across the beach and selling ice creams. From that moment I had loved cars, and had driven on and off ever since. Whenever my brothers needed someone to take the wheel while they sat in the back doing business, I had done it. I had a great friend whose father was a policeman, PC Renouf. He had quite a hard reputation, and he knew I was driving underage because I used to wave to him as I drove past, but he never reported me.

I'd even tried a motorcycle. My brother used to have a tuned-up Triumph Tiger 70. I remember coming back from school one day and saying to my friend, 'Come on, let's go up to Egypt Woods to check on our tent at the campsite!' We used to have this little tent there, in the woods on the north of the island, about five miles away. I pinched the motorbike, got him on the back, and headed for Queen's Road. That's quite a long hill, which heads north, away from St Helier. I revved it up, opened the clutch, and screamed away up the road. At the top I slowed down a bit, turned around to talk to my friend, and he wasn't there! I turned around, rode down to the bottom of the hill, picked him up again where he had fallen off, and up we went again. I remember going through Sion Village at about sixty miles an hour – there was no speed limit in those days – and I got into a bit of a speed wobble, when the front wheel just swings from side to side uncontrollably. I throttled back, slowed down, and it just got worse, so I opened it up to go faster and that calmed it down. It was the first time I'd ever ridden a motorbike! We got to the campsite and back with no trouble but on the way home I was really flying. Just before our house I pulled it into a great big skid, and BANG! The tyre wore through, and the inner tube exploded. I put it back in the garage and left it there, I didn't tell anyone.

I had to have fun like that occasionally, because I was starting to work really hard. I was sixteen years old, and we had to be loading the fish vans up at about six o'clock. We had a big store, the size of a three- or four-car garage, and then these great big refrigerators at the back. That was where the fish was stored. I'd have to go in there, select what I needed, carry it to the van, and make sure it was all ready to be sold. It was smelly, dirty work, and to be honest I hated that side of it. I didn't have proper overalls, just a big old coat to try to keep my other clothes clean. To fill our own stores up we'd have to put in an order with the wholesaler, and the catch would arrive on the mail boat. It had come all the way from Grimsby, where we got a lot of our fish from. We had to go down with our vans, and we'd watch as they unloaded it. It came on a great big pallet, and they used to lift it off with a crane. The man in charge would be counting it off, 'Reynolds, nine boxes,' then we'd sign for them, split it all up, put the boxes in the vans, and then take them back to our stores. I didn't enjoy it at all, but it was the family business and I was earning a good wage with my brothers.

Once the vans were ready, we'd have a quick bite of breakfast then we'd be off on our rounds. Our customers were all over the island. I'd drive about from one place to another, selling them whatever I could. The back of the van was set up like a little shop, with a till and a set of balancing scales. Of course the different types of fish were all worth a different amount, and that could change from day to day so I had to remember it all. Sole might be four and six a pound, while cod might be one and ninepence. But I soon got used to it. After starting at six in the morning, by the time I'd done my rounds, got back and cleaned everything up, it would be six in the evening. We took sandwiches with us and ate while we were working, no time for a proper break at all. Luckily it was only a four day week on the rounds, Tuesday until Friday. Monday was a cleanup day at the store, and Saturday was a day for cleaning and servicing the vans. We took them to Smith's garage on Stopford Road. We were all very proud of those vans. They were blue with mauve mudguards. They had 'Reynolds Brothers' down the side, with a painting of a salmon.

I was proud to be earning my own money too, and I was learning how to spend it. It meant that I could slip into a pub every now and again with my mates – underage of course – for a quick beer, and stand my round. In those days no one took much notice of that. I could buy my own clothes as well, ready to go out for a dance on a Saturday night. I remember buying a pair of winkle-picker shoes, and I thought I was it. Until they crippled my toes of course and I had to stop wearing them!

One Saturday night we went to see a friend of mine whose folks ran an antique shop in New Street, right in the middle of town. In the window they had this great big cocktail bowl, with all the little cups around it, and a little ladle. We all decided we'd fill that up to make punch, so we all turned up with a half bottle of something. I brought half a bottle of whisky, and someone else brought a bottle of advocaat, someone else had some liqueur ... So anyway, it all went into the bowl, and we mixed it all up. It was horrible! All I remember is staggering back along the road, trying to find my way home. I was so young, I didn't really drink much at all, so a couple of tumblers of that stuff really finished me off.

Smoking was very popular in those days too, especially for men. You could buy single cigarettes then, big ones, for a penny. Quite a few of my mates smoked, and I had the odd one or two. But I wasn't that interested, I never smoked much, until I joined the army a few years later.

I wanted to save my money anyway – to spend on more important things. Bumper cars. Just down the end of New Street, past where my mate's antiques shop was, there was a bumper car track permanently set up. It was electric, with these cars fitted with big rubber bumpers, and the aim was just to crash into your mates as hard as you could. The design hasn't changed much really, the tall electricity mast came up from the back of the car and got its power from a sort of network of power lines overhead. It was noisy, with the electric motors going full pelt, and all of us shouting our heads off as we chased each other and had big crashes. Of course, loving cars as much as I did and being a bit of a thrill-seeker I loved it; it was great fun.

I was having a pretty good time really. Work was hard, and took up a lot of hours in my day; but I was young, and had plenty of energy. I was always ready to go off and find the latest adventure, the next bit of excitement, and I had plenty of mates to do it with. I had a great family, a secure job, and a nice place to live. I thought my life was fairly well set. I was so busy with all of that, that I didn't really pay much attention to what was going on in the outside world, even though one of my brothers had joined the army. But while I was busy selling fish and playing bumper cars, Hitler had been getting ready for war. He had a huge army, navy and air force, even though he wasn't allowed to under the terms of the Armistice after the First World War. He'd marched into Czechoslovakia and Austria, and was getting ready to start a new war which would send me away from my lovely home of Jersey, and then into the biggest adventure of my life.

Chapter 4

NO GOING BACK

It all began when I went on a trip with my friend Roy Duval. It was the third of September, 1939, I was sixteen and the sun was out. We decided to head to the west of the island, to St Brelade's Bay. We used to like going to Tam's Pantry, a place on the beach where you could get really nice buns and ice creams. We were waiting in the queue, and they had the radio on; and that's where I heard that war had been declared. The Germans had invaded Poland, and Britain had demanded that Hitler should withdraw his troops at once. Of course he didn't, and Chamberlain had no choice but to carry out his threat and declare war. I remember the two of us thinking, 'Wow, how exciting!' because all kids think that war's fantastic, don't they?

But the adults in Jersey weren't so stupid. After all, thousands of them had gone to fight in the First World War, and the ones who came back knew what war was really like. They also realised that Jersey could potentially be a target for the Germans. Everyone suddenly started to live very cautiously. No one wanted to spend any money, no one bought new cars or started any building work on their homes. They were waiting to see what might happen. Life went on, but people became more and more careful, especially when the Germans occupied Poland easily and then invaded Holland and France in the spring of 1940. We used to listen to the radio to follow what was happening, I think everybody did. People knew it was only a matter of time before they got us.

My brother Charlie was in the Hampshires, billeted on the mainland, and my brother Sid had joined up soon after war was declared too. Luckily for them, neither of them was called on to go to France with the British Expeditionary Force. The BEF went to try to defend France against the Germans, and just got steamrollered. They had to escape from the beaches around Dunkirk, and the army lost so many men and so much equipment it was a disaster really. We heard all about it on the radio, but we were glad that Sid and Charlie were safely in England. It was an eerie time to be in Jersey. The whole island fell quiet, silent; there was nothing going on, but there was so much tension in the air. Everyone was worried what might happen. The big question everyone was asking was 'should we stay or should we go?' It was a really hard time for Jersey people. They wanted to stay, to look after their homes, it was their island and they were proud of it. But everyone knew that once France fell, the Germans would come over pretty quickly and try to take Jersey like they had taken all those other countries. We faced the same dilemma. Should we stay, to look after our home and our business, or should we go, and risk losing it all?

In the middle of June my mum made the decision: we were going. My two brothers were in England, and so were my sisters, and she wanted to be with them. I really didn't want to go, because I was settled in Jersey, and a lot of my friends were staying. But she insisted, 'No, we are going.' We headed down to the harbour to try and get on a boat, just like hundreds of other Jersey people who were leaving because they didn't want to fall under the Germans. There were queues of them, all waiting at the harbour for the next boat to take them to the mainland. And because we'd all left in a hurry, we couldn't take much with us, hardly more than the clothes we stood up in. I remember one well-dressed man standing next to a really nice motor car, trying to sell it or give it away to someone because he was leaving. 'Somebody give me pound for it,' he was saying. But we were all heading off too. My brother George wanted to stay though, because he'd applied to join the RAF, and was waiting to hear if they would accept him. His wife was pregnant too, so he wanted to look after her. He drove us down to the harbour. I remember queuing up, and one of George's friends came to see us. He used to work in the fruit and veg market, and went about with crates of fruit that he used to sell from his truck – just like we did with our fish. He brought us some fruit for the journey. We had a tray of cherries, and that was all we had to sustain us while we were on the boat. It was a filthy dirty little collier, which would often be used to take Jersey Royal potatoes off the island. But this time there were no potatoes, just evacuees, packed into the dirty black hold of this little boat. We were there all night, no other food or drink, no sanitation, just this tray of cherries which we passed around. I think everybody had a few of them, and it kept us all going.

We sailed from Jersey at about five in the afternoon, and didn't get into Weymouth until six the next morning. We spent the whole time stuck in the hold, and didn't know where we were until we arrived. When we got off the boat, the authorities there put these tags on us, to show we were evacuees, and told us to wait to be allocated a billet to stay in. But my mum said, 'Right, we're not staying here!' and pulled the tags off us. She wanted to go to London, to see my sisters. We got on the train and nobody stopped us. It was 22 June, 1940. My birthday.

When we finally got to London, to the Walworth Road again, I hated it. It wasn't fun like it had been a few years before, it was just dirty, smelly and unpleasant. I stuck it for a few days, then on 28 June I said to my mum, 'I hate this, and I want to go back to Jersey!' I decided I was going to go down to the station the next day, to see if the mailboats were still going to the island, and I would have got on one if they were.

But that morning, just before I headed off, we heard on the radio that Jersey had been bombed and machine-gunned the day before, and people had been killed; some of them around the harbour where I used to play. Soon after that the first troops arrived, and the island was occupied. That was it; there was no going back. We later found out that my brother George had waited too long for the RAF. He was caught there, like so many of our friends.

So I had to knuckle down and get used to life in London again. I had to earn my keep, so I became a fruit and vegetable seller. It was with Kingston's in Herne Hill, right opposite the railway station there. I earned two pounds a week, and I started every day at six in the morning. I didn't really know my way around London very well, but I bought a map and learned quite quickly. I went out on deliveries all round London, and to other shops. One of the people I used to deliver to was called Mrs Joyce; she was Lord Haw Haw's mother! His real name was William Joyce, and he was a famous traitor. He used to broadcast on the radio from Germany, to try and spoil morale at home, and for the soldiers serving abroad. I remember during the Blitz his broadcasts used to begin, 'Morning rats! Come out of your holes!' If the people of London could have got hold of him they would have shot him, I'm sure. His mother didn't want anything to do with him.

The owner of the fruit shop had two delivery vans, old Morris Tens. I drove one, and this old boy drove the other. But he was too old and slow, so half of his round got piled onto my van! Eventually the boss said, 'If you do all the orders I'll give you two pounds, ten shillings a week.' So I did, and sometimes I didn't finish until eight in the evening. I'd take the van home, where we rented a garage in the area called Manor Place, under some railway arches. Each morning I'd get up, drive to the shop, load up the day's deliveries, then get out on my rounds. Sometimes if the shops needed more stock I'd have to go to Covent Garden, which was still a fruit and vegetable market. I can remember the porters there used to carry about ten twelve-pound trays of plums balanced on their heads! I couldn't believe it. The market was full of stalls selling all sorts of things, some would specialise in plums, apples or bananas, there was always a lot of noise and bustle. It's all changed now of course, it's just a tourist trap. I went back there for the first time since the war when I was invited to Buckingham Palace; but I'll tell you more about that later.

Life settled down for a while, and I got on with working and trying not to miss Jersey too much. Hitler had won every battle; he'd taken over all the big countries in Europe, and his soldiers were marching up and down the streets of Jersey. Everyone knew the war would last for a long time, and I could feel people tightening their belts and saying, 'Right, this is it, we have to be prepared to suffer and work to make sure we win.' London, of course, was right in the middle of it all, and everyone was feeling very patriotic.

Everyone knew that Hitler wanted to attack England, and there were preparations going on everywhere. The Home Guard used to go marching about with broom handles because there weren't enough rifles, people dug trenches in the parks in case there were air raids, and we all had to carry our gas masks. There really was an air of expectation; people were worried about what would happen but they were determined to fight. In the end it was the RAF who did most of the fighting to start with. They fought off the bombers who tried to take out the airfields and radar bases on the south coast, and Hitler realised that he wouldn't be able to invade us as easily as he thought. But that's when things got far more dangerous for us, because he decided to bomb London instead.

I can remember the day the first bombs fell. I was out on deliveries in Streatham, and it was about seven in the evening. I heard the roar of engines and looked up. The sky was just black with German planes, and the bombs started to fall. The docks were already well alight. I finished my orders as quickly as I could, and drove home like a mad thing. When I got to Camberwell there was a policeman directing traffic, but he was panicking a bit and not doing it very well. I knocked into a cyclist and buckled his front wheel, and I can remember him going mad about his wheel while half of London was on fire from the bombs! The policeman told him to move off sharpish.

I got back to the garage and put the car away, then headed for the flat where my mum and sisters were. The planes were dropping incendiary bombs, which would just burn and burn, and one of them had landed in the builders' yard close by. It had set fire to one of the garage doors. There was a big pile of sand there so I just scooped up as much as I could and managed to put it out. Then I ran towards the flat and heard an old lady shouting, 'Help me, help me, there's an incendiary bomb on my roof!' But I couldn't stop, I wanted to see if my family was all right. I got to the corner and a bomb came whistling down. It landed on the pub just over the road and exploded with a huge roar. The pub was blown to bits, and the blast threw me about twenty yards down the road. I landed, covered in dust and debris, quite close to the entrance to an air raid shelter. A warden in the doorway saw me and pulled me inside. It was really frightening – the noise was terrific, I was completely disorientated and I didn't really know where I was. When I sort of came to, the warden told me I should stay, because more bombs were falling and it was really dangerous outside. But I wanted to get home, to get to my mum and my sisters. As soon as my legs would support me, I left the shelter and headed down the road to the flat. They were all sheltering in the basement, and luckily the flats escaped that night. But of course that was only the first night, and there were many more to come. I'll always remember the smell of cordite from the bombs, and also from the anti-aircraft guns which were firing away as soon as the bombers arrived. Every time a raid ended you'd go outside and the smell of it was really strong. You'd be tripping over bits of shrapnel and empty shell cases, as well as all the rubble from collapsed buildings. There was loads and loads of it. As the Blitz continued, I began to know what to expect. You'd look up and see barrage balloons all over the city, and if it was a night raid the search lights would be playing all over the sky. The sirens would howl – it's a sound which goes right through you. They would go up to a crescendo, then fade away, then go up again, then down – and you'd know the planes and bombs would come soon. You'd start to hear the throbbing of all those engines, the anti-aircraft guns would start pounding away, then the first bombs would fall, screaming and whistling as they fell to the ground. Sometimes you'd see the searchlights home in on one particular bomber, and then all the guns would open up on it. We saw a lot get shot down, and every morning the BBC would tell us how many had been hit. One night Mum and my sisters had gone to a shelter in Waterloo as a raid started, and I was late back from work. The bombs were falling as I ran towards the shelter, but it was already full and they had closed the doors. I had to plead with the warden, and tell him my family was inside, and he let me in. We were all crammed in, hearing the explosions outside and feeling the place shaking. After it finally finished, the sirens came on again, but this time just a long drawn out wail. It was the all-clear.

Another time I was out delivering and came round a corner to find a huge hole in the road. A bomb had fallen right next to this great big dust cart, and blown it up into the air. It had landed on top of a great slab of roadway, and was balanced at an incredible angle, closing the road completely. That was often a problem for me, as a delivery driver. Often I'd find that roads had been closed because of unexploded bombs. I'd have to stop at the end of the road, then walk down with a parcel to make sure the customers got what they wanted. There were lots of bombs that didn't go off, perhaps because they had been sabotaged by slave workers in the factory.

I used to drive everywhere quite fast because I was doing two rounds in one go. Once I came flying round a corner while there was a raid going on, hoping to get the deliveries done quickly. But as I got round the corner I couldn't believe what I saw. There was a huge hole in the road right in front of me, and the bomb had broken the gas mains which ran under it. Flames were coming out of the pipes and blowing up above the crater. I slammed on the brakes, skidded on some of the debris which was scattered all over the place, and somehow managed to stop just a couple of feet from the hole. Just a bit further and the whole van would have fallen into this great big burning pit. I jumped out and ran to the closest air raid shelter, which was just opposite the hole. You had to dodge round the blast wall to get to the door, then in through a narrow doorway. It was about the size of a long, narrow living room. There were about thirty or forty people inside. To my horror they were all dead – killed by the blast. Some of them were still sitting there, and even looked quite peaceful. I ran back to the van, reversed, and got away from there as quickly as I could. I took another road and got on with my delivery.

The raids were constant; they were at us all the time. I remember once the bombs just fell all day. The all-clear never sounded.

Perhaps the worst sight I saw was in a school playground. I had to go there to make a delivery, but I couldn't get in there because it was full of all sorts of vehicles. I realised they had used any car or lorry they could find to pick up dead bodies, and they had all been brought to this school. The ground beneath them was a lake of blood. What a sight for a lad of seventeen. The smell was awful too. There was nowhere to bury these poor people, and they had just been left there while the authorities decided what to do with them.

For a while we were lucky, and our home remained untouched. But one night late in September there was a big raid. We heard the sirens going, and the guns started off, so we said, 'Quick, let's head to the shelter!' On the way we knocked on the door of a young lady in the same block as us, who had a young baby. She was going to stay, but we said, 'Come on, come with us!' She did, and we all ran as quickly as we could to get to the shelter. Once we were in there, the sound of the bombs and the way the ground shook was frightening. Eventually the doors opened, and we could hear the all-clear. But what a mess everything was; the whole area had been hit really badly. There was rubble, broken glass and dead bodies everywhere. When we got home, we found our luck had run out. Our block had been smashed to pieces, and our flat had been turned to ruins. You could see into the front room, and the floor was hanging out with everything falling away from it. I managed to climb up what was left of the concrete stairs, but I found all our bedrooms had just vanished. The floor started giving way every time I moved, so I had to get out. A short time before, I'd bought a new suit, and I could see the jacket hanging off the ivy which was wrapped high up around another part of the building. I had to leave it.

My brother Charlie was on leave at the time, and had left his rifle in the flat when we left to go to the shelter. He'd asked me to look after it. I picked my way through the ruins and found it amongst all the rubble. I remember putting it over my shoulder and stumbling off down the road. An air raid warden stopped me and said, 'Right, where are you going, give me that!' But I explained to him that it belonged to my brother, who was on leave, and I was going to try to find him. I think he felt sorry for me, and he let me go.

I had nothing else left, apart from the clothes I stood up in and two shillings and sixpence in my pocket. I found my family, and we were all in tears. It wasn't just us though. There had been a lovely old couple who used to run a shop just on the corner of the flats, and they never used to go to the shelters. They would stay in the shop and hide under the stairs. But they didn't survive the bombing that night. My sister lost everything she had. She had to go down to a depot nearby, where people from America and Canada had sent emergency supplies of food and clothes. She came back with a shirt for me which was so big it would have fitted me four times!

We went to my aunt's, which was a couple of roads away. We had to sleep every night in the Anderson shelter, a corrugated roof you put over a hole which you had to dig in the garden. One night I slept right through a heavy raid because I was so tired. When I woke up we found the whole of the next street had been blown to bits. A huge land mine had landed on it. My aunt's house had been damaged, but not too badly. I tried to carry on working, but the bombing was causing so much disruption to the roads and the trains that I just couldn't do it. The authorities decided we would have to be evacuated to somewhere outside London. When I told my boss, Mr Kingston, he said, 'Don't you worry, come and stay with me!' I think he wanted to adopt me, but I said I had to stay with my family. We were off – to somewhere I'd never been before.

Chapter 5

MAN'S WORK

I don't remember leaving London, but I do remember that we were all very sad. None of us had anything left, and we had nowhere to go except where the authorities put us. I think we got the train away from the noise and destruction of London, and in some ways it was good to get away from the fear, the sirens, the crash of bombs and guns, and the uncertainty of whether you would still be alive the next day. The place we ended up in was completely different! It was called Whalley, in Lancashire, half way between Burnley and Blackburn. It was a beautiful, peaceful little village, with a bowling green in the middle where I first learned to play. We were billeted in a hotel which was called the Judge Walmesley. It wasn't being used as a hotel, but was taking in evacuees like us. It's still there. It was quite big inside, and we had rooms right at the top. It was a very busy place. As well as me and Mum, there were my aunt and her husband, and their three daughters all sharing the space. There weren't many facilities though, and all Mum had to cook on was an old paraffin stove. Everything she made tasted of paraffin!

I managed to get a job in a garage in the village, helping out with car repairs, so I kept up my interest in motors. The old boy who owned the place had a sideline going in ammunition too. Out the back he had

I made parts for these guns – a 25-pounder on the beaches of Normandy

equipment for milling and turning parts for shells and gun carriage hubs for twenty-five-pounder guns. There were eight or ten of us working there, on these great big machines. I didn't really make friends there, because they were Northerners and kept quite closely to their own people. They knew I had come from London, and they didn't much like Southerners. I did a lot of work helping them though, and we used to put in twelve-hour shifts at night. I can remember starting work in the daylight, working through the night, and when I finished it was broad daylight again! We hadn't completely escaped from the German bombers either. They used to fly over the village sometimes as they headed for Manchester. There was one occasion I remember really clearly. In the garage there was an inspection pit. It was a hole with a couple of strong planks over it, so you could drive a car onto the planks and then get into the hole to look at the underside of it. Suddenly we heard the roar of engines, then the scream of bombs coming down. Of course I reacted just like I had in London, and ran towards this pit and dived into it. They all stood there laughing at me! I set them straight, I said, 'If you'd been through the Blitz like I had then you wouldn't be standing there!' The bombs had landed about a quarter of a mile away in the fields, and no harm was done. I'm sure they weren't actually attacking Whalley, because it's such a tiny place. It was probably a straggler jettisoning his bombs on the way back from an attack.

I got quite fed up with working in that place, because I got very tired and it wasn't good for my skin. I was making the threads for tracer shell plugs. When you milled the parts, you used a machine which turned very fast, and the parts got very hot. To cool them down you had to plunge them in a big container full of oily water, which used to splash all over you. I got a nasty rash from that, and had to go to the doctor. He got me released from that job. He had to be involved because it was classed as essential war work, and you couldn't just walk out on it. Once you were registered on essential work like that you were meant to stay there, and nobody could move you from it. You couldn't even be called up!

I did want to do something useful for the war effort though. I was looking through the jobs section of the paper when I saw they wanted volunteers to work in Liverpool, repairing damage done by the bombing there. The company doing the work used to organise coaches to pick their workers up from all over the area, and one of them came from Burnley right through Whalley. So I signed up for that. A whole coachload of us would get picked up at about six in the morning, and they would drive us to Liverpool. We'd spend the whole day working there, and get the coach back late at night. It was a long day, and I seemed to spend half of it on the road!

Liverpool had taken quite a battering from the bombs, and lots of buildings had been destroyed by blast. We got busy on the simple repairs, where doors had been blown off or windows smashed. We'd just replace them with bits of plasterboard – a quick repair. There were some terrible times though. I can remember one place, a co-op shop. They used to have a stock warehouse below, and everyone used to go down there when the air raid sirens sounded. One night it took a direct hit, with three hundred people inside. Nobody survived, and they couldn't even get the bodies out. We had to work close by, and the smell was just awful. Luckily for me, at such a young age, I never had to deal with bodies close up.

The people I worked with were much older than me, men who were too old to go into military service. But I got on well with them, even though I was a Southerner, because they could see I was a hard worker. Eventually the authorities realised that I would get more done if I was actually billeted in Liverpool, so they got me a little place there, which I shared with one of the older blokes.

I had already tried to join the services though. I was nearly eighteen years old, and was desperate to do my bit. My brothers were already in the army, but I fancied the RAF, so I put my name down for it. I spent three days at an RAF base in Cardington, where they made me do all sorts of tests – navigation, intelligence tests, things like that. The doctor there passed me as completely fit, and he said my eyesight was perfect for night fighting. But it wasn't to be, because when they eventually interviewed me and asked me what I wanted to do, of course I said I wanted to be a fighter pilot. That's what we all wanted to be in those days – they were the glamorous heroes, the Brylcreem boys, and they always got the nicest-looking girls! I was fascinated with aeroplanes too, their speeds and excitement. But they said, 'Sorry, we don't need fighter pilots at the moment. What we do need are gunners, to fly in our bombers.' But I'd seen hundreds and hundreds of bombers shot down over London, and knew that wasn't for me! So I said no thanks, I wanted to be in a plane that I could manoeuvre, to make my own decisions. They said, 'OK, go away and think about it, and we'll look to see what other jobs we can give you.' But it never happened, because two weeks later I got my call-up papers to join the army. It's just as well really.

If I'd been an air gunner, I probably wouldn't be here today. They sent my call-up papers to my billet in Liverpool, and believe it or not I was posted back to Whalley!

Just outside the village there was a manor house which was a training centre for the artillery, and that's what I had to learn about. I was in an artillery training company. Twenty-five-pounders, the same guns that I had been making parts for earlier! My joining-up date was 2 February 1942. I remember it really well because it was freezing cold, and snowing. They kitted us out in the morning, and most of it didn't fit me at all. The uniforms we were given were covered in a white powder, to stop you getting lice. The first thing we all did was beat our uniforms to get rid of it, and we all ended up covered in the stuff! In the afternoon they decided they we would make a start on the PT, or Physical Training, course. It started snowing again as he took us out, and we stayed out until about five in the evening, when it was already dark. We were only allowed to wear a singlet and vest and we were all absolutely frozen. Of course the showers were no good because all the other platoons had already got back and used up all the hot water! So two of us decided we'd have a go under the cold water anyway, because we were so dirty. We had a good clean, and it turned out that we were the only two that didn't get a cold as a result of it. It didn't bother me too much because I'd been used to playing in the sea when I was a kid in Jersey, and I got used to it quite quickly. Most of the other blokes in the group were from around Whalley though, and the sea was a long way away for them in those days.

The training was hard, and the discipline was harder still. There was a curfew; if you had any time out you had to be back to camp by 11.59 or you'd be in trouble. One Saturday night I didn't get back until half past midnight. I'd been to the local dance which they used to have in the village hall. I met this girl there, and after the dance finished I'd taken her back to her place, and she lived three miles away! I lost track of time, as you can imagine, and had to sprint as fast as I could back to camp. But I was half

In uniform

an hour late.

They couldn't let me get away with it, and I got seven days Confined to Barracks. They made me march at running pace with a full pack on around the drill square for an hour every day. It was agony! They gave me all the horrible duties. I remember them showing me a huge mountain of potatoes, which I had to peel with three or four other blokes who'd been naughty too. It was all right though – we were all young and we had a bit of a laugh about it.

It was quite rare that we got to go out and have good times or dances. For a start, we had hardly any money. My pay was two shillings and sixpence a day, seventeen and six a week. That wasn't enough to really enjoy yourself on, even if you were allowed out of barracks after curfew! I'd send seven and six back to my mum, because she didn't have any income at that time. My brother Charlie did the same. That left ten shillings, and by the time you'd bought all your soap, razor blades, cigarettes and things, there wasn't much change out of ten bob! I can remember going into the village one Saturday, when I had some time off, and I could only just scrape enough together for one half of beer.

We had to do a lot of marching. *Left right, left right* all the time, and we had to learn to be proper soldiers. I remember the first fifteen-mile march we did. We'd been issued these real old-fashioned army boots, which were tough and really uncomfortable. We had these big thick woollen socks, but the problem was that they wore out really quickly. About three quarters of the men dropped out before we finished, and I think I might have been one of them! The blisters on my heels were so sore I just couldn't go on. I hated those boots, but still had to keep them shiny. The sergeants showed us how to make sure the toes were like glass. You had to use blacking, spit, and the back end of a toothbrush to rub it with. You had two pairs of boots actually: the ones you had on, and the ones which were ready for show. Every morning when you got up you had to make your bed and display all of your equipment on it. Your clothes all had to be neatly folded, your greatcoat too, and all the buttons had to be nicely polished. Even if we'd spent the whole day out on exercise in muddy fields, you'd have to come back and make sure all your things were ready for inspection the next morning. One of their favourite training places for us was this big lake. They made us wade across it as fast as we could, carrying our rifles above our heads so they didn't get wet. But they'd dug these big holes on the bed of the lake, so every now and then your foot would go down into nothing and you'd have to try to stay upright – either that or you'd go down, rifle and all! There was a big hill we had to run up at full pelt, then a steep drop on the other side. They made us jump over it, to get us used to falling over, I suppose. A similar exercise was just a trench filled with mud which you had to get across. We would crawl up and over nets, or underneath them as they weighed you down. The sergeants would be firing a Bren gun with live ammunition right across you, to try and make it feel realistic. One bloke put his bottom too high in the air and got a bullet up the backside! It was such hard work, but you just had to do it. If you didn't you could be punished. One of our blokes got sent to the Glasshouse, which was the army prison. When he came back, he said to us, 'Don't get sent there lads, whatever you do – it's a terrible place!' so I always did my best to do what they told me.

Reveille was at six, no matter what time of the year it was, and you had to get outside on parade to be counted. Once I was so tired I pulled on a pair of pants and just threw my greatcoat on over the top before I went out on parade. There wasn't time to dress properly.

There was hardly any hot water, and we always shaved in cold. I must have cut myself a thousand times. That was one thing I never got used to, and one of the first things I bought when I left the army was an electric razor!

Of course in those circumstances you inevitably had bullies, and we were no exception. There were those who made other people clean their gear and fetch and carry things for them, but I never got involved with that. They did try it on with me, but I told them to bugger off and they left me alone.

One thing I had a go at was boxing. I thought I was quite good at it, and I beat about six of them. Then they put this bloke who was a professional against me, just to see what I could do, and he walloped six bells out of me! I tried my best but I'd never had any training or anything. That was the last time I tried boxing, I wouldn't bother with that again!

We had to learn formation marching too, when you all stay in step, *left right, left right,* and turn and manoeuvre together. I got quite good at it actually, and I think I was becoming quite a good soldier. We learned to fire our rifles, fight close up, use bayonets and throw grenades. I remember there was a round pit with about half a dozen of us in it, with a sergeant showing us how to pull the pin from a grenade and throw it properly. There was one stupid idiot who dropped the grenade inside the pit, and we all panicked and jumped out to run away. The sergeant had seen it all before though, and he picked up the grenade, chucked it away, and yelled to us, 'Quick, get back in!'

I never really thought about how we would use this training, to actually kill people. We did the usual attacks on sandbags with our bayonets, all the bloodthirsty stuff. It was very hard, all of it. They trained us as infantry, as well as artillerymen. Another thing we had to do was go through gas chamber training. They used something called DM gas, which just made you feel as though you wanted to die. What you had to do was go into this room in a concrete bunker with a gas mask on, then they'd fill it with this gas. Then they made you take your gas masks off, so you could see what it was like to be gassed. It was awful, your nose would run, your eyes would stream, even your teeth would ache. Your whole body would ache. Once when they made us do this I made sure I was at the back of the crowd and tried to get away without taking my mask off. But the sergeant saw me, and came over and pulled my mask off my face. I can remember getting out into the fresh air and feeling just awful. But it was important training for us, we had to know how to deal with a gas attack. On the front of our trucks we had a yellow circle which would change colour if there was poison gas around. The concern was that the Germans would fire gas shells at us, and if we weren't quick enough in getting our masks on we would be useless to fight back when they attacked us. Luckily for us it never happened.

After all of this they passed me as A1 fit, which meant that I was as fit as I could be. I think my upbringing in Jersey helped me a lot, because I was always running about, riding my bike or swimming, so it gave me good basic fitness.

Eventually, after my basic training, I was posted to the 151st Ayrshire Yeomanry, a Scottish regiment. They were based in Godalming in Surrey. On my first morning with them I went to the canteen and they had these great big containers of porridge. Lovely, I thought, I love a bit of porridge. When I took mine back to the table, I asked the blokes there – who were nearly all Scottish – where the sugar was. 'What for?' they asked. 'For my porridge!' I replied. 'Don't be stupid,' they laughed, 'we put salt in ours!' And that's how I had to eat it. Yuck.

We went for our artillery training to Sennybridge in Wales, in the Brecon Hills. That's where we learned how to fire the guns. There were all sorts of different duties involved in firing a twenty-five-pounder, which is a big gun. First it had to be towed into position, and of course with all my experience driving the family vans I volunteered to be the driver. They had already given me the driving test, which I had passed easily. When I first joined up there had been about a hundred of us in this big shed, and the sergeant asked us if any of us knew how to drive. Of course I put my hand up, and I was the only bloke that did. 'Well,' he said 'you won't need to drive anywhere for a while. So in the meantime, stay behind and sweep out the shed!' Never volunteer for anything in the army! But they noted my experience, and soon after that they gave me the test.

I was trained on these big trucks, three tonnes with canvas roofs. They took the roof down, then made you reverse between these barrels which they had stacked up on the ground behind you as obstacles. I got it down to a fine art, and was able to drive up to the right spot, slam it into reverse and get right between the barrels really quickly. Then we learned how to manoeuvre with the guns hitched up behind us, on what we called quad trailers. We were trained by these two corporals who used to put the fear of God into us. They divided us into two teams, one under each of them, and used to make us race between the obstacles. When it was my go I made sure I put the fear of God up them with my driving instead! I was fully qualified by the time I passed out of basic training.

When we got to Wales and were learning how to use the guns I would tow the gun to the right place, and back it up so they could unhitch it. Then once it was all ready for firing, my job was to load the shells and close the breech of the gun. Another bloke had to aim the thing, and my crew was lucky, our aimer was really accurate and hit the target every time.

I never had time to get to know many of these chaps though, because my brothers came and 'claimed' me for their outfit - the Royal Army Service Corps.

Charlie had been in the Corps first, and had claimed Sid from the Hampshires, and now the two of them claimed me. The system was that if you had a brother serving somewhere else in the army, you could get him to join you in your own division. Our unit was quite a new one; we were the 310th Company of the Royal Army Service Corps, Guards Armoured Division. They were based in Cleveland in Somerset. You could look across from the high ground of our camp and see Wales.

It was a nice change for me. As well as being reunited with Sid and Charlie, it was a nice place to be. We were actually billeted in houses near the seafront, and it really reminded me of my home in Jersey. It was great. I joined a platoon which was driving three-tonne lorries, carrying ammunition. I even had a go for a short time at being a despatch rider on a motorbike. I should have learned my lesson after my first motorbike ride in Jersey! One night I was going with seven or eight other riders to Weston-super-Mare for a beer, in the driving rain. The road wasn't surfaced with normal tarmac, but this sort of pinky stuff which was very smooth. We got to this huge left-hand bend, and as we hit it every one of us lost our motorcycles! We were all spread across the road, but I managed to get away from my bike as it slid because I didn't want to get hurt.

On another manoeuvre, in the August sunshine, I was screaming along ahead of the column with my shirt unbuttoned to keep me cool. Suddenly I ran into a swarm of wasps, which managed to get right down inside my shirt and started to sting me. I had to make a very quick stop, whip my shirt off, and try to get rid of them!

Me as a despatch rider

Later on that same exercise I lost the convoy. I had to try to catch up, so I worked out what I hoped would be a great short cut. I started flying off down this little lane, doing about sixty, when I came to this sharp 's' bend. Of course at that speed there's no way I could stop in time and I ended up in a field with the cows!

57

Perhaps I was lucky that my career as a despatch rider came to an end. I was offered the job of driver to a captain. We went out on manoeuvre again, and the major in charge had this Humber Snipe. We only had an Austin 10, which was no match for it. The exercise began, the major set off down the road, and my captain shouted, 'Follow him!' So I put my foot down, but so did the bloke who was driving the Snipe. We had a real race, cutting all the corners and skidding the tyres. I was hammering the little car, chasing him as fast as I could, down all these little roads and lanes until the Captain shouted, 'Stop, you mad bugger!' We went, more slowly, into this little village where he ordered me to stop outside the pub. He bought me a beer while he had a very stiff whisky! I certainly had the competitive driving spirit, even in those days.

Other exercises could be more complicated. They'd take us out in the middle of the night and drop us in the middle of nowhere on foot; we'd have no idea where we were. They'd give us a small compass and we'd have to find our way back to camp as quickly as we could. We weren't given any rations, and I can remember raiding the turnips in someone's field, eating raw turnips at about one o'clock in the morning.

I must have been doing well though, because they sent me on an NCO course to Catterick. It was a seven-day course, which I passed, so I could sew a stripe on my sleeve. I learned the basic words of command and was qualified to instruct recruits in basic training. It wasn't all plain sailing though. I went out with this girl on a night off, and I was late back again. We'd found a barn together. I thought I could sneak back in, but when I crept to my bed I found the regimental sergeant-major sitting on it waiting for me! 'Hello,' he said, 'where have you been?'

'Well, Sergeant,' I said, 'I've been out with a land girl.'

'Did you get what you wanted?' he asked.

'No!' I said.

'Well you'll bloody get it tomorrow, I can tell you!'

The next morning, he said to me 'Right, I want you to drill this lot of recruits. You see that big heap of stone chipping over there? Go and stand on it and you can drill them from there.' Of course the heap of stones was so far away from the parade ground that by the time my command reached them they were on the wrong foot! It was impossible to do it no matter how hard I shouted.

Despite that setback, by the end of the week I had qualified and was back with my own company. One of the first things I had to do when I got back was drill the platoon with my brothers in it! I can remember standing in front of them, taking a big breath to shout a word of command – and nothing came out! I had dried up. Of course they laughed at me but I got my own back once my voice returned. I had a real go at them: 'Pick up your feet Reynolds!' and so on. I'd been promoted before both of them.

I didn't manage to keep my stripe long though. We were sent on yet another exercise – up north near Scarborough. We'd been stuck in the same field for about three days with nothing to do, and nothing going on. It was what was known as a 'petrol-less' day, when you were meant to be unable to use the vehicles. But I had saved a special pink chit from the previous week, which gave you permission to be on the road on that day. I got a pen and altered the date on it, from a one to a four, and said to the boys, 'Come on, let's go for a drive into town!' We got into Scarborough, and had a good time. But on the way back we ran into some Military Police, who we called MPs. They had a roadblock across the road, and we couldn't avoid it. They asked why we were driving on a petrol-less day. So I showed them the chit which I'd altered, and they spotted that I'd changed it. I was in trouble, and the decision was that I would lose my heard-earned stripe. I was gutted about it because I was earning twenty-six shillings as a lance corporal, as opposed to seventeen and six as a private! I had been able to send Mum some more money, and had a bit more to spend on myself, but I lost it. They never offered me another chance until I was in Germany.

Chapter 6

TRUCKS, DUKWS AND AUTOMOBILES

While I was busy training there was real war going on in other places. Churchill had decided we needed to take on the enemy somewhere, so a proper fight had developed in North Africa. We were fighting against Rommel and the Africa Corps, and they were really good.

By the middle of 1942 things were getting pretty desperate there. Rommel had pushed on a long way, and just wanted to take El Alamein, which was quite close to the coast. If he had, then the Germans could have gone right through to Cairo. But the Allies fought back hard and managed to stop him; and then they pushed him back.

Of course we all heard about this back in England, because it signalled an important victory for us, after the Allies had been beaten so many times elsewhere. What it meant for me and my brothers and my mates though was a really really hard exercise.

The high-up officers studied what had happened at El Alamein, and realised that a lot of our success had been down to the massive artillery bombardments. A lot of those had been done by twenty-five-pounder guns, just like the ones we were trained to use.

They told us that one of the units there had managed to keep firing for three days and nights without a break. The gunners, they told us, kept on firing, and the supply chain kept on working to bring them ammunition. So, they said, we should be able to do the same. I remember my major saying, 'If they can do it, you can do it!' And that set the scene for some very hard work for us, as they came up with an exercise to see if we really had it in us. We headed off into the English countryside, and it all began.

I drove all sorts of trucks in the army. This one is a Ford V8

I was still a lance corporal then, in charge of a group of six trucks. They were big three-tonne Bedfords. My job was to keep an eye on them all, and also to drive an ammunition truck myself. We had to pretend that the guns were firing, and we had to keep them supplied with shells.

When the exercise started, we had to be prepared not to sleep, and only to stop for refuelling or repairs. We simply had to keep going.

I had to pick up a truckload of ammunition cases from base, drive miles to the gun site, help to unload, drive back to fill up again, and so on. Another lot would pick up the ammo we had dropped and take it right back, so really we were just moving the same shells around the whole time! Each of the cases weighed a hundredweight, and they all had to be shifted by hand. We kept going for as long as we could, for three days and three nights. Gradually it started to wear us down, and it was really hard just to keep your eyes open and concentrate on the road, especially because you were doing the same route over and over again, in the light or in the dark. We lost one truck, then another, then another, from my group of six. I remember one bloke just fell asleep as he was going across a little bridge, which had a very low parapet on each side. The lorry drove right up onto the parapet, and started to topple over. He must have woken up with the crash, and jumped out of the cab just in time, because it went right over into the river. Eventually it was just me left. My strongest memory is just how easy it was to drop off as soon as we stopped for fuel or a quick bite of food. I can remember clearly the despatch riders coming past and banging on the door, 'Come on Reynolds, wake up!'

I don't know how I stayed awake, but I did, all the way to the end. I can't remember the end of it at all, I was so tired, I have no idea how we all ended up. I suppose I must have felt responsible, being a lance corporal, and I wanted to make sure that at least one of my group actually made it to the finish. I do remember the major saying, 'Well done, Reynolds!' but that's about all we got for completing it.

It turned out to be very good practice actually, because when we got to Caen in 1944 we had to do exactly the same for real when the boys were trying to take the city.

We did manage to have some fun when we were on exercise though. I remember on one occasion I wasn't driving, but manning the mounted Bren guns we had on the trucks to protect us from aircraft. We were driving along a road and there was a party of prisoners of war working in the fields next to the road. Just for fun I swivelled my gun round towards them and they were so scared they all just broke and ran for it! We never had much respect for the Italians. Back at base we had pictures of all the different types of enemies we might face. It was so we could learn what their uniforms looked like, and their different units. There were Germans and Japanese, who all looked quite threatening. The one of the Italian had the body facing forwards, but the legs were on backwards so he could run away!

It was at about this time that I met Monty. We were at a base in the north of England when he visited. He must have recently finished the campaign in the desert and was taking over the 21st Army Group. We had to get up very early to make sure we were all shiny and immaculate, and we stood on parade for hours. Monty arrived and marched along our ranks, as we stood to attention. He came down my rank and stopped right in front of the man next to me. He didn't make much of an impression on me at the time, and when he'd finished talking to my neighbour he just moved on. It's a shame, because I would have liked to tell him my story, how I had come from little Jersey and been blown up in the Blitz. Still, the atmosphere that day was incredible, as every part of the Guards Armoured Division was there, and there were lots of bands playing. I remember marching off from there, and the sound was wonderful, all of us marching in step, with the bands playing as loudly as they could.

Another bit of fun was the rugby match that the major organised. He decided it would be good for morale if we had a game – and he announced that he would play too. It was great – as soon as he got the ball all the players of both sides piled on top of him and squashed him flat! He never suggested another game after that! None of us liked him very much. On a Saturday afternoon, when we were hoping to get out for some free time, he'd have us all on parade. It would finish with an inspection. Now his hair was quite long, down to his collar, long for a soldier. But he'd march down the parade line behind us, and slap each of us in turn on the back of the head, or he might tap you on the shoulder and say, 'haircut.' The problem was, there were only two barbers in the whole of the company. So while two people could go and get their hair cut, he'd make the rest of us keep marching around the parade ground until it was our turn. I hated it. Before I joined up I had quite long hair, and I really liked it. The training unit I was in, and the Ayrshire Yeomanry, had been happy for it to stay like that, but this bloke insisted I had a haircut as soon as I joined. I felt like I'd been scalped! They used these hand-operated shears, not electric ones, and the result looked awful.

We carried on training, and the tide of the war was turning. As 1943 wore on, we could see that the Germans weren't having things their own way any more. While I practised driving my truck and loading up ammunition, the Russians were fighting hard to push the Germans back. By the end of the year the Germans were retreating almost everywhere. We had beaten them in the desert, and we kept hearing about the big bombing raids which were going across into Germany every night. I think we all knew though that we'd have to fight on the Continent, and that meant we'd have to invade somewhere. At the time though, we didn't have a clue where that might be, or when.

The first clue I had was when I was chosen to go on a training course on the Isle of Wight. I went to learn how to waterproof vehicles so they could be driven into the sea, and other skills. Bearing in mind my previous adventures in canoes and skiffs, it was quite brave of them to send me. I had a few adventures there!

I was sent to Ryde, where they had a big selection of military vehicles. They told us we would be taught how to take command of a landing craft, how to drive a floating jeep called a DUKW, which we called a 'DUCK', and how to load and unload our trucks from a pontoon. We learned all these things, and a lot more besides.

We had to do a lot of our exercises at night. One night, I was on a small landing craft in the middle of the Solent, and everything was completely dark. No one was allowed to show a light anywhere because of the blackout. We were drifting around, and I didn't know where the hell we were. To make things worse the fog started rolling off the land, and we got completely lost. Luckily I wasn't in charge; I was being instructed by an officer. We could have floated out to sea, and no one would have known. Eventually we heard a noise coming from the land, and we headed towards that and found our way back.

Another time I was learning to drive a DUKW in the Solent, this time in the daylight. There were eight or ten of us taking it in turns. It's a funny-looking craft, with a rounded hull and wheels underneath so you can drive straight up the beach and onto a road. There I was, with the instructor watching me, trying to get the hang of this thing. The Solent was a busy place though, and all sorts of different organisations were using it. The RAF was one, and it had some pilots in old Fairey Swordfish torpedo bombers practising making dummy attacks on the warships there. They were so old-fashioned they were biplanes, and very, very slow. They were nicknamed Stringbags. But one of them took a bit of a shine to me, floating about in my DUKW, and decided to have a go at me. I watched him turn and make his approach, and he flew straight towards my little boat. He had a torpedo mounted under the fuselage, which may or may not have been a dummy. But I wasn't expecting him to drop it! He must have pulled the lever because the torpedo dropped from underneath him and headed straight for us. Seven of the blokes jumped overboard and started to swim for it. I was driving though, and that was one thing I was good at. I threw it into reverse, full throttle as fast as I could. The torpedo came down, down, down, and *splash*! landed just a few feet off the front of the boat. It was such a near miss. The plane then came round again, really slowly, and because it was an open cockpit I could actually see the pilot laughing his head off. I had to go round picking my mates up, and I was laughing at them.

I went on an American Liberty ship too. They were like merchant ships, which the Americans built and sent to us to use as supply vessels. Hundreds of them were sunk by submarines in the Atlantic. We were using them to load and unload from. I went to the galley to get a drink, and remember seeing loads of cockroaches running all over the floor. The exercise was to go out to the Liberty ship on a pontoon, offload supplies from it, then drive the pontoon back to shore.

Learning to operate pontoons was really tricky. They were just big flat landing spaces with motors on. You used them to go alongside ships or harbours so you could load or unload trucks on them. A mate of mine was steering one towards the quay, with six or eight vehicles on it. As he got close, he caught the front vehicle on an obstacle, but it didn't stop the pontoon moving. First one vehicle, then the next, then the whole lot were pushed right into the sea! Luckily for me again, someone else was in charge at the time. In fact there were so many of us doing all the training that there was always someone around.

The waterproofing was quite a challenge. You had to make sure that water couldn't get into the engine of the vehicles, so that when you drove off the ramp onto the beach it would be able to keep going if it got wet. What you did was put a breather pipe into the petrol tank, and seal it with mastic. That's a sort of rubber solution which would set quite thick. The pipe meant that as you used fuel some air could get into the tank and you wouldn't get a vacuum stopping the flow. Then you'd do the same to the carburettor so it could draw in air. The rest of the engine got covered with mastic too, so water couldn't get to the plugs, the dynamo, the distributor, or any of the working parts. We fitted longer exhaust pipes too, so the ends would be above the water. We didn't bother about the doors or windows; we just had to be ready to get wet! They told us that when we got dropped on the beach from a landing craft we would be in about six feet of water, and we would just be able to drive straight down the ramp and onto the beach. Once we were off, the ship would be lighter and could float off again, to go back and pick up more vehicles and men.

I remember particularly working on a quad gun truck, a huge thing with wooden sides at the back and great big tyres. They were designed to tow artillery and carry ammunition. I did a good job of it, and felt confident enough to test it. When it was my turn I drove it down the ramp and onto the beach. I kept going into the water. And so began another of my maritime disasters … I drove out a little way, and everything was going well. The problem was, the tide was coming in fast, and the water quickly got very deep. I didn't stop though. There was nothing in the back to act as ballast, those great big back tyres acted like flotation tanks, and the whole of the back end lifted off the bottom. All the weight of the truck was in the front, with the engine, so the back started going up and up and I couldn't go anywhere! I had to be rescued. That was embarrassing…

As all these preparations were going on, we were working really hard and some of us needed to let off steam. One of our men couldn't wait to get into a fight, and didn't care who it was with. I remember we were in a pub in Thetford in Norfolk when these Americans walked in. Now, Americans weren't always very popular with British soldiers. They always had the best uniform, the best food, and the best presents for the girls. This fellow from my platoon really hated them, and he started a proper fight. He smashed a glass on the counter to use as a weapon, and really went for them. There were glasses, boots and fists flying. I got out as quick as I could; I've never been a fighter like that.

The Americans weren't a bad lot though. For a while we were in a camp next to a Flying Fortress airfield, and you'd see them all through the fence smoking and eating for all they were worth. So me and my mate went in, met a few of them, and asked if we could buy a few fags. One of them took us back to his billet and showed us a box full of stuff hidden under his bed. Not just cigarettes, but chocolate, chewing gum – you name it, he had it. And he just gave us some packets of fags, and wouldn't take any money. They had so much more than we did. Mind you, we didn't like the cigarettes much – they were Lucky Strikes!

Chapter 7

INVASION

As D-Day approached we were sent to Southampton to join the rest of our forces who were getting ready for the big day. We were stationed in a camp on the edge of the town, on the common. We were all still worried about being attacked, and we dug deep slit trenches that we could hide in if there was an attack. I can clearly remember a Doodlebug coming over, and me and my mates were in that trench in seconds! They were terrible things. We could hear them coming over because their engine was quite noisy, and then suddenly they would cut out and it would be dead silent. They had been given a calculated amount of fuel so that they would crash down into a particular city. You'd never know where they were going to land, and it was terrifying. Later in the war, near Arnhem, we were billeted in a house which was near a graveyard. This Doodlebug came over and landed right in the cemetery. It blew a crater in the ground right where all the bodies were buried, and blew the roof off our house too. Everybody hated those things.

That camp on the common was so busy. There were so many men, trucks and machines, from all over the place – Brits, Yanks, Canadians, and all of us were keen to be off and get on with it. We hung around there for three or four days, and had to stay with our vehicles, just waiting. We weren't allowed out of the camp in case we gave anything away. We spent the time just worrying about what we were getting into, and how our families were. I was still in touch with my mum up in Whalley, and while I was in that camp she sent me a parcel. Inside was a lovely cake and a jar of Brylcreem. The only problem was, the jar had smashed and the Brylcreem was all over the cake! It didn't stop me and my brothers though. We scraped it off and ate as much as we could. I saw them as much as possible, which wasn't too difficult because we were in the same company. I was in 'A' platoon, I think Sid was in 'B', and Charlie was in 'C'. We'd try not to go in the same truck together just in case it got hit.

Eventually the camp started to empty, and we realised the invasion was on. We weren't scheduled to go in on the first day, and we watched all these other blokes head off, wondering if they would be all right, and what it might be like for us.

It was more than two weeks before we finally got moving, because they had so much to get across the water, and so many battles to fight there. We were to be used as reinforcements for the big push across France. They thought the main battles around the beaches and inland would be over, and that we would be mobile all the time. But while we were waiting, they had got bogged down because they hadn't managed to capture Caen, the big city a few miles inland from the beaches. That's where we would end up. We were all ready to go, but a big storm blew up on 19 June, which caused all sorts of problems. That lasted for three days, while we sat by our trucks and waited for the word to go.

We finally headed out of our camp in the trucks, down to the Solent. There were lots and lots of our trucks, three-tonners, all of them waterproofed and ready. I had taught the people in the company what I had learned on the Isle of Wight, and every truck was carefully sealed up.

We were loaded on to a Liberty ship, and as we were getting under way this huge bombing raid flew over us. It looked like a thousand Flying Fortresses, all on their way to bomb the Germans, probably in Caen.

For some reason one of them broke up in the sky as we watched, it just disintegrated.

On the boat it was rough, but we had to look after ourselves. They gave us these cans of food, which we had to warm up on this steam pipe which ran along the deck. Some of us were lucky and got these cans which heated themselves up when you pulled a little ring pull on the top.

Of course we were just one of loads and loads of ships, all full of blokes like us, all sailing down the Solent and nervous as hell. We were given our invasion money, and soon the card schools began, we were all at it. There was nothing else to do. Some people hit the beaches rich, some of us were broke. And there wasn't much else to do with the invasion money anyway, because we didn't find many places that would take it. Just one, when we sneaked into Bayeux for a drink.

We ended up playing even more than we expected, because after we were loaded up they decided to hold us in the Solent for an extra day because of the weather. It still hadn't settled after the big storm. That wasn't very nice, and we had to find ways to relax. We were all expected to sleep in these hammocks down in the hold, like the navy boys. There was this one chap in the company who was a bit of a bully. He was a boxer, a big bloke. But when he got into his hammock for a sleep in the afternoon, me and my friend Willmore got some cord and tied it to each side of it. We pulled it to and fro, swinging it all over the place, and he woke up and was violently sick! Luckily for us he was too sick to chase us.

The storm had destroyed some of the Mulberry Harbour, an artificial harbour just off Arromanches, which they had been using to bring supplies in to the beach. That was in the middle of the British beaches, but we were headed for Sword Beach, at the eastern end of the Allied beach head.

They transferred us from the Liberty Ship onto a really big landing craft, a Landing Ship Tank or LST. They lifted us up with a crane, and moved us across. I'm not sure what time we landed, but it was certainly daylight. We could see the French coast getting closer and closer, and we could see the evidence of the landing. There was a destroyer which had been completely smashed, and its bows were sticking up out of the water. The sea was full of bodies – sailors from that ship and from some of the others nearby. There was so much debris on the beach: blown up DUKWs, smaller landing craft which had been shot to bits, it was carnage. We could see all this as we made our run in to shore. It made us all very nervous, but we got ready to land anyway. I was a sort of freelance driver at that time; I didn't have a truck of my own, so I jumped on someone else's. The driver was this young lad who I'd taught to waterproof his vehicle. The ramp went down, and off he went. But he hadn't done his job properly, and as we drove into the water the engine just stopped. So we sat there, up to our chests in water, and had to wait for a tank to pull us out!

Once we got to the shore we managed to get the truck going and made our way inland. We had to cross a minefield which they told us had been cleared. But there were still signs all over the place which said *Achtung Minen*, which put us all even more on edge.

We made it through though, and we were off the beach. There weren't many houses in our sector, but I do remember one really clearly. It had a balcony on the first floor, and there were these little girls on it, waving at us. We got onto the right road, carried on a little way, then we had to pull into a field next to a line of fir trees. We were ordered to pull scrim nets over the trucks to camouflage them, and then stop for a while. That was it. We were in France. It was 22 June, 1944. It was my birthday, four years to the day since I left Jersey as the Germans invaded.

SUPREME HEADQUARTERS
ALLIED EXPEDITIONARY FORCE

Soldiers, Sailors and Airmen of the Allied Expeditionary Force!

You are about to embark upon the Great Crusade, toward which we have striven these many months. The eyes of the world are upon you. The hopes and prayers of liberty-loving people everywhere march with you. In company with our brave allies and brothers-in-arms on other Fronts you will bring about the destruction of the German war machine, the elimination of Nazi tyranny over the oppressed peoples of Europe, and security for ourselves in a free world.

Your task will not be an easy one. Your enemy is well trained, well equipped and battle-hardened. He will fight savagely.

But this is the year 1944! Much has happened since the Nazi triumphs of 1940-41. The United Nations have inflicted upon the Germans great defeats in open battle, man-to-man. Our air offensive has seriously reduced their strength in the air and their capacity to wage war on the ground. Our Home Fronts have given us an overwhelming superiority in weapons and munitions of war, and placed at our disposal great reserves of trained fighting men. The tide has turned! The free men of the world are marching together to Victory!

I have full confidence in your courage, devotion to duty and skill in battle. We will accept nothing less than full victory!

Good Luck! And let us all beseech the blessing of Almighty God upon this great and noble undertaking.

Dwight D. Eisenhower

Chapter 8

INTO BATTLE

The field we were in was a big one, with a thick row of trees down one side. The Germans were still around, and unfortunately still interested in us. There were quite a lot of shells coming over, and we ducked every time they landed nearby. The problem was that the Allies hadn't managed to capture Caen quickly after D-Day, which they were meant to do. It wasn't very far away, but it was a great big city with defences which were getting stronger all the time as the Germans brought up reinforcements.

On the day we arrived, Operation Epsom had begun. That was a big attack to the south of Caen, to try to cut off the Germans in the city. They still hadn't managed to take Carpiquet airfield either, and there was fighting around there too. All of this was going on just a few miles away from us, but because of the delays with the weather our unit wasn't ready to go straight into the action.

So there we sat, in our field, listening to the boom of the guns and feeling nervous about the shells which landed close by. We each had a little cardboard box which contained our twenty-four-hour ration packs. They didn't have much in them really: chocolate, a couple of cigarettes, iron biscuits and a bit of tea. But as we brewed up and ate them they gave us a bit of comfort.

As the fighting was going on elsewhere, we were put to work doing other things. There was a ruined chateau nearby, which had been blasted to bits in the fighting. It had been a German HQ, but now it was just rubble. We were sent there to carry supplies for the pioneers who were fixing the road. While they were loading up the trucks, I went for a wander in the gardens of the chateau with my friend 'Willy' Willmore. There was this little woodland area which we explored, and we came across a German bunker which was a real arsenal of guns and explosives. There were guns, hand grenades, booby traps, mines, you name it. We played around with all the bits and bobs we found, chucking stick grenades across the fields and into the stream, until we had to get back. We saw the pioneers and got our trucks, and drove them to collect more stuff. When we got back for another load one of the chaps said, 'What on earth were you doing down in the woods earlier?'

'Not much,' we answered, 'Why?'

'Because the whole place blew up after you left!' he said. We went to have a look, and where this great big bunker had been was just a huge, smoking hole in the ground. It must have been booby-trapped, and we had got away with it! We hadn't been warned about that sort of danger because we had only just got to France. We had to be more careful.

'Willy' had become my best pal. Most people in the army had a friend like that, who you would rely on, and be able to talk to if things were tough. We did everything together. He had a narrow face, fair hair and protruding teeth, and came from the Midlands. We used to take the mickey out of some of the other men in our group. One was 'La Sen', who was from up north, Lancashire I think. He never used the word 'self'. He'd always say, 'I was there all on me sen,' or 'All by me sen,' so we all called him La Sen. And there was a Scottish fellow, whose name I forget, who was really mean. He'd ask you for a cigarette, and you'd never get one back. He'd always creep back to his bunk, get one out from a packet under his pillow and say it was his last one. Eventually no one would give him one.

Willy and I shared one particular interest: girls. Whenever we went out we'd go together, looking for pretty ladies. He was quite successful too! We could only afford to go out once a week while we were in England though, and it was usually to the village hall where they would have a dance. There were always quite a lot of girls there, and soldiers too. It got quite competitive sometimes, but once you got a girl you held on to her in case someone else nicked her. That's what led to seven days confined to barracks for me when I walked one home for three miles and was late back.

I was punished in another way for my interest in girls. At the time, the fashion was for wide trousers, and when you're young these things matter. So I took my battle dress trousers, slit the seam up the side, and sewed in another piece of cloth in a 'v' shape to open them out a bit. Of course it was only a matter of time before an officer spotted me, and it was, 'Sort those trousers out!' It had taken me hours to do, and I pulled them apart in moments.

But chasing ladies stopped when we got to France, and we had to get on with work. Our only real diversion was playing cards. We loved that, and played all the time. Once on exercise we'd thrown all the chickens out of a chicken coop because it was so cold outside, and we got down to a serious game called 'shoot' while everyone else ran around. We played for cigarettes, because none of us had any money. I won a lot of them in that game, and I remember they were almost black because they'd been handed around so much.

We didn't have much time now even for cards though. One job we had to do was to take supplies to and from the beach head. There was still some of the Mulberry Harbour left in the sea in front of Arromanches, and we went to pick up things from there. I can remember driving down the hill to the beach, and out onto the harbour. I thought it was an extraordinary thing, a real achievement. What they had done was to build these huge floating concrete blocks, which they then towed across the sea and anchored into place next to each other to make a completely new place for ships to dock just off the shore. It was linked to the beach by pontoons. You'd drive down the long hill, then out onto the pontoons to the harbour itself. Supplies, usually ammo, would come out of the big ships, onto smaller pontoons, and then be ferried across to be loaded onto our lorries. The remains of the harbour are still there today.

It wasn't long before we found out just how dangerous France could be. As the army advanced, there was a real rush among the supply troops to find and occupy good spaces to turn into supply dumps. As we started to advance on Caen, we found a field and decided it would be perfect for our ammo dump. As soon as we got there we started to dig our holes, a sort of slit trench arrangement to protect us if there was any firing. That was always the priority, as soon as you got anywhere: get your hole ready! But the Germans were still strong at that point, and started shelling again. They sent over what's called a creeping barrage. That's when the carpet of shells sort of rolls towards you, so you know what's coming. We crouched down low in our holes as the barrage went over us, and it was very frightening. I had a bottle of Calvados in my pocket which I had got from a French farm, and we drank a lot of it that day! Luckily we didn't have ammo in our truck, because we were only there to grab the space for later. Normally we could have had all sorts of ammunition with us, from small arms to tank shells or even twenty-five-pound artillery shells.

I'd got the bottle of Calvados from a farmer when I'd gone to barter for some eggs. I did the deal, and he gave me a cup of coffee with some Calvados in it, as well as a bottle to take away. It was strong stuff, and it really affected me. I remember going back to our command post, a small tent. The sergeant said they had just captured an enemy soldier. It was the first living German I had seen, and I was suddenly overwhelmed with anger. For the first time it really hit home to me – these bastards had taken over my home island of Jersey, captured my brother, blown our home in London to pieces, killed all the lovely people in those flats, and done all these other terrible things. I thought it was time for revenge.

'Where's the bastard?' I asked, 'I'll shoot him!' For a moment I really meant it.

The officers knew I had been drinking Calvados though, and they didn't let me anywhere near the prisoner; in fact they put me under arrest until he'd been moved and I was sober. I still don't know if I would have done it.

I remember all the Germans I met had a particular smell about them. I don't know whether it was from their uniforms or from themselves, but it's one of the smells I remember the most from the war. Mind you, I don't suppose we smelt too nice either! When we were in action, or pushing hard, we didn't often have time to get properly clean. I remember forty of us having to share the water in a cut-off five gallon can to wash and shave. By the time we'd finished it was thick! We'd have to wash our own clothes and socks whenever we found water, but there was really nowhere to dry them except in the truck. We often had no sanitation at all, sometimes just a hole in the ground.

Shortly after I met that German, we were in a field next to a stream, with a farmhouse just up the hill nearby. We went up to the farm again to get some eggs, because we were always on the lookout for them. We got our eggs, and headed back down to where the trucks were parked, down by the stream where there was a soft, flat grassy bit. I got out my cooking gear and started frying. Just as things were sizzling nicely I heard a gun fire a shell, and because I had never been shelled directly before I didn't realise it was coming straight for me. I just heard *BOOM! wheeeeeeeeee!* as it flew through the air. Then it landed, just a few feet away from me on the riverbank. Luckily the earth was soft, and the shell went into it, carried on spinning, and came out the other side of the bank before it exploded with a hell of a bang. It was another near miss for me!

We had very little time to relax while all this was going on, but I do remember getting punished for taking a trip to find a beer. We weren't far from Bayeux, and Willmore and I headed to the town on foot. It had been liberated quite soon after the invasion. We slid into the centre all right, and found a nice little cafe for a drink. There was a brothel next door, and the girls were trying to entice the MPs who were on duty outside to come in.

When we'd had a nice couple of beers we headed back the way we had come, to get back to our unit. But MPs had set up a new roadblock which hadn't been there on the way in. When they caught us we told them that we'd hitched a ride from a farmer who had dropped us in Bayeux instead of back at base, but they didn't believe us. They reported us to our officer. He gave us seven days confined to barracks, but he said, 'You know I can't actually confine you to barracks because we aren't at the barracks, we're in the field!' He wasn't really angry with us, but he had to show that he'd done something because we'd been reported by the Military Police. In the end we just carried on with our duties, and the punishment didn't really mean anything at all.

Around this time, part of our division was based to the north-west of Caen, while some units were involved in taking the airfield. That turned out to be a really bloody affair, because there were some fanatical Hitler

Youth in there, and they didn't want to give up in a hurry.

Soon the time came for the big push into Caen. The artillery was going to play a major role in getting the Germans out of the city. I had good cause to remember the exercise we did back in England when we stayed up for three days running ammunition to and fro, because that's what we did at Caen. It was another three days and three nights of constant shelling – bombarding the Germans around the old town with our twenty-five-pounders. It was a horrendous time, far worse than when we had done it before. This time the guns were firing constantly and the noise was deafening. There was no way you could have slept, even if you had wanted to. Back and forth we went, back and forth in our trucks to the ammo dump, then back to the guns, unload, back to the dump. The guns kept firing into Caen, smashing it to pieces.

When the attack finally stopped, Willmore and I looked for a place to shelter and maybe catch up on some sleep. We found this orchard with a German double slit trench running through it; it was part of the farmhouse nearby which had been blown to bits. The pair of us managed to get some old doors from the house, and put them across the top of the trench to keep us dry and protect us a little better. The earth which the Germans had dug out we piled on top of them. It meant we could crawl into our trench and sleep a bit, because we were just dog tired. But we were only in there for a couple of hours when the Germans retaliated, and came in with bombers against us as night fell. They bombed eight bells out of us. Having come through the Blitz in London and Liverpool, I could tell where aeroplane bombs were going to land. I heard the scream of these bombs falling, and I thought, 'This is it.' I knew they were coming for us. Six bombs came down into our little orchard, two of them either side of our slit trench, right on target. But none of those six went off! A lot of our trucks were hit though, and caught fire. We spent the rest of that night trapped in our little trench, because all the ammunition in the trucks was going off and there were bullets and shells flying all over the place. All sorts of explosions were going on because of the blaze of the trucks. And right next to us were these unexploded bombs in the ground! Poor old Willmore had it even worse than me. He'd got bitten to pieces by mosquitoes in his hole, while they left me alone. It wasn't until the morning that we managed to get out, and saw all the devastation around us, and the holes in the ground where the bombs had hit and not gone off. We couldn't believe we were still alive.

We got our own back though. As well as our three-day bombardment, our own air forces attacked the Germans in Caen. I remember watching Lightnings going in firing their rockets, then the Flying Fortresses going in in droves. The noise was just horrendous, you had the bombardment going on, the noise of the guns firing and shells exploding, the aeroplane engines and the bombs they were dropping. The ground just shook, and you couldn't hear anything else. But it did give us a bit of confidence. We thought the attacks must have smashed the Germans in Caen at last. They were clever though, and many of them had withdrawn just before the bombardment started. A lot of our bombs had just killed French civilians.

The main battle we were involved in was Operation Goodwood, which began on 18 July. We moved around the edge of the city, to get to the south-east of Caen, and the Guards Armoured went in as the second wave. Our tanks were attacking towards a village called Cagny, and we had to be right behind them carrying ammunition so they could rearm as quickly as possible. The bombardment before the battle started was colossal; they really threw everything at the Germans. Artillery and heavy bombers smashed up lots of enemy positions and tanks, which we saw as we moved forward. But it wasn't easy, and we were fired at a lot by the Jerries who had survived. We lost quite a few tanks and men in the attack, and there was smoke and explosions all around us. Our chaps in their Sherman tanks absolutely hated the German Tiger tanks which were around there. There was no way to take them out unless you could get them from behind and shoot them up the backside; they were just too heavily armoured. And the Germans had the best anti-tank gun as well, with the famous 88mm.

It fired these armour-piercing shells which would go straight through a Sherman. You'd see fields full of knocked-out Shermans, all with just a single hole through the turret. We'd stayed as far away from the enemy tanks as possible, because we were so vulnerable in our lorries full of ammunition.

Operation Goodwood was really tough for us, but it didn't finish off the Germans in Caen. They stayed fighting, and we were sent to help the Yanks further to the north-west. They were having a hard time seeing the Germans off in the area around Vire and St Lo, and our division was part of something called Operation Bluecoat. The Americans had launched Operation Cobra in that area a week or two before, but the Germans were fighting back against them. So what we did was to attack them from another angle, to take them by surprise and help to get them out of the western part of France, up to the Cherbourg Peninsula. That was a great battle for me to be involved in, because that part of France is one of the closest to Jersey. I can remember driving through St Lo after the battle, and on top of the roof of the railway station there was a smashed up Tiger tank.

It took almost until the end of July to get the Germans out of Caen, and they were pushed out of the city and into retreat. We weren't allowed to rest though, because the army had to keep chasing them. We turned back, away from St Lo to drive through Caen, and my God it was a mess. You couldn't put a pin between the shell and bomb holes. The roads were just rubble, impassable. We had to have a bulldozer in front of our convoy just to make any way at all.

Caen has a beautiful cathedral, which has been restored now after all the fighting. But as I came down the hill into the city I could see that it had just been ruined; the spire and everything was just a pile of stones. As we got closer I could see the doorway to the church, and there was a dead baby hanging from the door. It must have been killed during the bombing, and someone had put it there. That was very disturbing, and I can never forget it.

After we left Caen behind us, we were right in the front of the push, making the Germans retreat to the east. The Guards Armoured attacked and we went forward right behind them with ammunition again. There was no time to stop, to take a break or relax. Our orders were to keep going, and it was working. We knew we were doing well because we kept moving forward. While we were doing that, the Americans were mopping up the Jerries who were left on the west side of the invasion beaches. They all got trapped as we cut their army in two, and the Americans were able to wipe them out before heading over to help us.

All through this I'd been with my truck, driving, loading or unloading. We took it in turns to do the driving, although it's what I liked the most. You'd get right up to the front, the tanks would disengage the enemy and get into some cover where we could get to them quickly. We'd get right up to them and hand up cases of shells and machine gun bullets so they could get right back into it. We had to keep working until our lorry was empty, then get back to base to fill up again. The pace was frantic because we suddenly had the Germans on the back foot; they were heading into the trap of the Falaise Pocket with us chasing them.

Chapter 9

DEATH AND DESTRUCTION

We drove into the area known as the Falaise Pocket in the middle of the night, and fell asleep. When I woke up and had a look around, all I could see was bodies and wreckage.

Falaise was awful. The Germans were in full retreat, and weren't really able to defend themselves properly against being attacked as they ran. Our air force was at them all the time and they were squeezed into this little pocket of land with one road leading out of it. We drove through it as they went before us, and it was a total shambles. There were so many wrecked vehicles, so much smashed equipment and so many dead bodies all over the place. They had abandoned their horses, or used them for food; you'd see horses dead by the side of the road with great chunks carved out of them. I just wanted to get away from it as soon as possible, it was horrible. But at the same time we were quite elated because we had broken away from Caen and were moving so fast all of a sudden.

It was the beginning of a chase right across France and into Belgium. As usual we were right up at the front with the tanks, and we saw the aftermath of all the battles, although at this stage there weren't so many of them because most of the Germans were just running away. Our divisional commander was replaced as we began the push. There was very little resistance as we flew across France, and sometimes we'd go up to seventy-five miles a day. We kept our lorries going as fast as we could to keep up with the advance. Sometimes I'd be driving; sometimes I'd be in the passenger seat responsible for loading and unloading the ammo. If we were needed, we'd drive right up to the tanks or guns, pass them up the shells as fast as possible, and get away quickly before the German artillery found us.

There were always reminders of the war in places where the Germans had resisted. We'd see farmhouses smashed to bits, with dead cows and other animals lying outside and smelling terrible. There had been so much destruction that the French weren't always pleased to see us. We often meant trouble for them because we'd damage their property, or provoke a counter-attack.

When we got to Arras, near Belgium, there was a really angry atmosphere because the local people were turning on the 'Jerry bags,' the women who had collaborated with the Germans or been their girlfriends. They were shaving their heads and parading them about the town. The local FFI – the armed resistance – invited me and my mates to take part in a memorial service for the dead. We went to the monument just outside the town, presented arms, and fired a volley in respect. It was strange seeing the old trenches from the First World War there.

Just before we got to Belgium we stopped in a couple of villages that I remember clearly. One of them had a great big dance hall with a lovely old-fashioned organ. It was one of those where you put a sort of cassette in, pumped the bellows and it would play automatically for you. It had huge ornate pipes curling right up to the ceiling. They played it for us, and lots of the villagers came to dance with us. They were so excited about being liberated, and we had a wonderful party with them.

When we pushed on to the next village, Willmore and I pulled in for the night. We stopped at a farm, where the farmer gave us some Belgian money, thanking us for liberating them. That was very handy, because we didn't have any Belgian money at the time. We asked him to look after our truck, which was full of ammo, took the distributor arm off just in case anyone tried to steal it, and got ready for a party. He directed us down to the village, which was on a straight road, in typical French style, with cafes on either side. We went in for a beer, and found that the local girls were very friendly!

We were advancing so fast though, that we didn't have time to hang around. After being held up around Caen for so long, we were now flying across the country. On one of the roads I had a real coincidence. We were approaching Belgium, and the road as usual was scattered with vehicles which had been knocked out or abandoned. As we went up this hill, there was a huge amphibious troop carrier on the right hand side, which had run out of petrol. Then just a bit further up was a 1939 Flying Standard car. I stopped close to it, got out, and scratched a bit of the German army camouflage paint off it. It was maroon underneath. Now I don't think there had been more than one or two maroon versions of the Flying Standard exported from Britain before the war started, but my brother George had one, which had been bought by the Germans when they invaded Jersey. He'd bought it just as the war started, as a present for his wife Sybil. The chances of there being another Flying Standard of that colour in France were very slim, so it could well have been Sybil's car!

It was my division that liberated Brussels, on Sunday 3 September. That was quite a day. The Guards Armoured were in the forefront of the advance at that point. And what a reception we had! Thousands and thousands of people were on the streets, throwing fruit into our vehicles, chocolate, bottles of wine … they were all singing and dancing, shouting and cheering, jumping on our trucks and tanks, waving flags … and there were so many pretty girls asking for a kiss! I'll never forget the welcome the people of Brussels gave us.

We stopped that night just outside the city at a place called Rhode-Saint-Genèse. It's halfway between Brussels and Waterloo. After all the euphoria we still had to be careful, because we were told that there were

*Our hosts
in Brussels*

three hundred Germans in the woods nearby. We got a load of sandbags out of the trucks to make a little round emplacement, and got our Bren gun ready, in case any of them decided to make a move during the night. We always had sandbags in the vehicles on the floor, to give us a bit of protection if we drove over a mine. I was trained to be ready to defend myself if necessary. As well as being a driver, I had been trained on the Bren gun, and also the Piat. That was a small anti-tank gun, a bit like a bazooka. It wasn't much good though. By the time I got to Brussels I'd fired most of the guns we had around. It was quite a nervous night, because we didn't know if we were going be attacked. Another night without too much sleep.

It turned out that the people whose house we were camped out next to had been off to the centre of Brussels to find themselves a Tommy to bring home. They'd had no luck, but came back to find us camped out on their doorstep! They were fabulous people. They were a husband and wife, and very rich – he was an industrialist. The house was big and we ended up staying there whenever we could. They looked after us well, and really thought the world of us. They knew we liked a drink, so they kept us topped up with brandy and all sorts of things. If I'd seen a German come out of the woods I would have sworn there were six of him.

But that had to come to an end, and we were off to be part of Operation Market Garden. That was the famous 'Bridge Too Far' attack. Montgomery had come up with this hasty plan to make a fast crossing into Germany by taking three important bridges over rivers which led to the Rhine. Parachutists were going to seize them quickly, then wait for us to come and relieve them. The Guards Armoured Division, of XXX Corps, was going to be one of the leading British units to attack along a single road towards Eindhoven, Nijmegen and Arnhem. Monty thought it would be a quick way to get the war over with, because once we had crossed the Rhine into Germany we would be able to attack the rest of the country more easily.

We formed up on our start lines in good shape. We had our best battledress on, and the anti-lice teams had come around to clean us up. You had to stand there while they put a sort of pipe down your neck, and squirted in some kind of chemical to kill any infestation. All the trucks and vehicles were immaculately cleaned. We used rags soaked in petrol to give them a bit of a shine. The attack started, and we had perhaps twenty miles to travel to get into Eindhoven, which was our first objective.

The problem was that the whole advance, all the tanks, armoured cars, supply trucks and troops, had to go up one single road. The Germans could see exactly where we were going, and found it really easy to hold up our advance by attacking us from the sides. Once they had caused a traffic jam by stopping one vehicle either with an air attack, artillery or tanks, the whole lot ground to a halt. It took us a long time to cover those twenty miles, but we finally got into Eindhoven on 19 September at about six o'clock in the evening. All the houses in the town had their flags out to welcome us, and the people were really happy to see us. My unit had three sections: there was fuel, supplies, and my lot with ammunition. That was a lot of heavily loaded trucks to get through the town and onto the next objective, which was Nijmegen. We were really tightly packed in the centre of the town, hundreds of vehicles nose to tail, three abreast. We couldn't really move.

And that's when the Germans came in with their bombers, and blew us all to hell.

I knew the difference between German bombers and ours because the engines sounded different. British and American bombers synchronised their engines, so they sounded as though they were one single engine: *brrrmmmmmm*. But the Germans never synchronised theirs, so they sounded very irregular: *brrbrrrmmmbrrbrrmm* … and I knew that these bombers were German and heading right for us.

The bombs began to fall and trucks full of fuel and ammo started to explode, so I knew I had to get away as fast as possible. Just around the corner from where we were was an old public baths, and an old man called out to us to come and shelter there. He led us down some stairs and into the basement, below the bathing pool. I think it was where they heated the water and pumped it up into the pool itself. While we were in there, a bomb came through the roof of the building and exploded as it hit the water, right above us. Luckily it was a strongly built place, and although everything shook it didn't come through to us. If the bomb had damaged the pool, I'm sure we would have been drowned. There were so many bombs coming down, we were terrified.

Just as the raid was coming to an end, the officers came and got us all out ready to move off, but another plane came over. We all started to fire up at it, although I only had a Sten gun so I probably couldn't do much damage. My sergeant had the Bren gun. It flew straight down the road at us, very low, and we could see it very clearly. But suddenly it seemed to go out of control, and it crashed; we'd actually shot it down! My sergeant later got the Military Medal for that. I ran towards where the trucks were, to try to help, when another stick of bombs came down. One landed in the back of a three-tonne truck full of dynamite, which went up with a huge explosion. The force of it picked me up and threw me down the street, but luckily I wasn't too badly hurt.

Once the planes had gone, we looked around to see what damage had been done. Lots of our trucks were either completely destroyed, or were in flames. There was wreckage and debris, wounded men and dead bodies. We had to salvage what we could. I got to one truck which was so badly damaged by shrapnel that I could only get about five miles an hour out of it. We had to move as many as we could though, to save them from being lost. I drove it past all the others which were smoking and burning, but it was very hard to manoeuvre through it all. I came very close to a building which was well alight, and starting to collapse. Some of the debris landed on the canopy of my truck, and it caught fire. I got it as far as possible from the wreckage, then jumped out and pulled the canopy off, because there were three tonnes of ammo underneath!

We lost a hundred and twelve trucks in Eindhoven that day, and a lot of men. A friend of mine had tried to find shelter in a bungalow nearby, possibly after being injured. It caught fire, and was soon well alight. We tried to save him, but we couldn't get in; all we could do was listen to him scream. He was a nice lad, from Wales I think. More than two hundred civilians were killed too.

A while after that day I remember reading an account of the attack in one of the British papers. It had a photo of our vehicles in flames with the caption, 'German transport knocked out.'

After the raid we assembled outside Eindhoven to try to repair the trucks that were still serviceable, because we still had an important job to do. We worked all day and all night. I was changing a wheel at about four in the morning when I saw a group of soldiers approaching, which looked like a German patrol. I grabbed my gun and was just about to give them a blast when someone shouted, 'Hold it, they're Yanks!' From a distance the Americans' helmets looked very similar to the Germans'. That was a very close call. By then we were all trigger happy because of the big air raid and a lack of sleep.

We weren't the only group to have suffered from German attacks. They knew that we were advancing down a very narrow road, and had no protection on our flanks. So they were firing into the sides of us all the time and we were always driving past knocked-out trucks and tanks. They were very clever; they would stop the vehicles at the front and back of the column to make sure it couldn't move out of the way, and then shoot up the rest of them. In Eindhoven they had let the tanks go through deliberately before attacking us, so that the tanks were left with no supplies. They had put up a strong fight in France, but were even more determined in Holland.

After we got through Eindhoven we headed towards Grave, in among the rest of a long convoy. By then we'd had no proper sleep for days, so we had to stop to rest, then try to catch up. There were German counter-attacks all the time along the road, and we actually got cut off near the village of

Oss. That was a frightening time, and we had to survive on our own for three days. We were billeted at the house of the local dentist, whose wife was about to have a baby. He had a fifteen-year-old daughter too. Luckily, although we were cut off, there wasn't any fighting around us and we could just wait to be freed. We had plenty of ammo, but didn't actually have the guns to fight anyone off. I remember scavenging for German rations which had been left around. We ate a lot of tinned black bread, and drank a lot of ersatz coffee!

Once our tanks arrived we were back on the road, pushing to get to the bridge at Nijmegen. The American 82nd Airborne was at the bridge, trying to take it from the Germans, but they had almost as much trouble as the British in Arnhem. Eventually the Guards Armoured arrived there and helped in the battle.

After the war it was quite controversial, because some people said that we had delayed too long. The Americans pushed across the river in little boats just down from the bridge to take it from the Germans, and they wanted us to go straight on towards Arnhem. British paratroopers were there, trying to hold the last bridge against the Germans, who were trying to take it back. But our commander had ordered us to rest because he knew how tired we were after the last few days. I think stopping was a big mistake though, in hindsight. We should never have stopped. It cost us thousands of lives. At the time we didn't realise that, it was just good to have a breather without any fighting. Unfortunately the Germans used it as a chance to regroup.

There was still fighting going on when we got to Nijmegen, and the tanks were starting to get over and into the country on the other side. Soldiers were fighting in the woods very close to the bridge, and areas around the northern side were still in German hands. We would load up with ammunition at the dump on the southern side of it, then we'd have to take it across to the tanks who were trying to fight towards Arnhem. That was really dangerous, and we would fly across there at fifty miles an hour

The bridge at Nijmegen that we crossed under fire

The bridge as it looks today

with all the ammo in the back, hoping to dodge the firing coming from the Germans. We'd wait behind a building and get ready to charge across one at a time. I remember watching the truck before me going over, then counting down: 'three, two, one, GO!' and giving it full bore, no slowing down, all the way over. They had artillery and heavy machine guns all zeroed in on the bridge because they knew we would try to use it. I drove like hell over that bridge, with my foot right down on the floor, just praying they wouldn't hit us.

On the other side, when we were stopped, they would fire moaning minnies at us; they were huge mortar shells which made an awful, frightening noise as they dropped towards you. The noise went straight into your nervous system. As soon as you heard them you would drop flat. They made the earth shake when they landed. We'd have to wait for a signal to come back across the bridge again, and it was full bore to get back to safety. Then we'd have to load up ready for the next run. I don't think I even had time to have any fear or emotion about it all; just get on the bridge, get your foot down, get to the other side and get your work done. We all had jobs to do.

When we weren't loading or carrying supplies we hid behind the ruined buildings at the bottom of the hill next to the south side of the bridge.

One of our most dangerous missions didn't involve ammunition though. About five miles north of the bridge at Nijmegen was a village called Elst. It was only a small place, but there was a German headquarters there and it was the centre of a violent battle. It was full of infantry, guns and tanks, all dug in and ready to fight.

The reason it was so well defended is that it was on the main road, almost exactly halfway between Nijmegen and Arnhem. If we wanted to reach the British airborne troops who were trying to hold the bridge at Arnhem we would have to go through Elst, and the Germans knew it.

There were shells landing in it all the time, as the tanks and soldiers fought among the ruins. The problem was that the people who lived in the

Above: The church at Elst today.

Left: Villagers rushed out of these doors and into the back of my truck while we were under shellfire.

village hadn't been evacuated, and lots of them were still there. They had gathered in the church, which was the biggest and most solid building still standing. We were ordered to go there and collect all the people we could, then bring them back to our lines for safety.

We unloaded all the ammunition we had in our trucks, and braved the bridge crossing at full speed again. There were about ten of us in our convoy. There were bombs and shells and bullets flying all over the place, but we managed to get over. Then it was a five mile drive over roads covered in shell holes, being bombed and shot at, to get to the village.

By the time we got there most of Elst was in Allied hands, but the Germans were still about and it was being very heavily shelled.

I remember getting to the square where the church was, spinning the truck around, dropping the tailgate and reversing full pelt up to the doors of the church. There were lots of families in there, women and children particularly, who were waiting for us. We literally threw as many people as we could into the back, and took off again back towards the bridge. But there were shells landing all around, especially aimed at the road we had come down. Those were the longest five miles I had ever driven, and we really just flew back over that bridge with all the villagers getting shaken around in the back. We made it though, and they got to safety behind our lines.

All the time this was going on, there were other battles being fought around and in front of us. Supplies had to be flown in because the only road between our bases and the front was full of our tanks and trucks. I remember seeing hundreds of Dakotas flying over us to drop ammo, food and fuel to units who were fighting further away from us. Sometimes the 'chutes wouldn't open and they would come whistling down close to us, sometimes in the same field. They came in useful later on …

Once a glider came down very close to where we were, and the American troops in it ran out firing their machine guns at us! I jumped into a ditch, thinking it was dry, but it was soaking wet inside! It took a while to persuade them we were friendly.

We wanted to go faster, to get on to Arnhem, but we had to be really careful. The Germans had mined the ground alongside the road, so you had to watch where you went. One of our trucks came off the road and into a minefield. A sergeant went to try to guide them out again, and trod on a mine which blew his leg off. The Germans were brilliant at booby-trapping and mining places, and you never knew what could happen. By that time we were used to seeing death and injury, and it was something we had to deal with every day. We used to play cards all the time to try to take our minds off it. Once we were sat under a tree playing when there was a dogfight above us. An American fighter was attacking a Messerschmitt which was already in a bad way and heading for the ground. But the American kept on firing, and the bullets were getting close to us. One of them must have ricocheted off a tree or something, and it hit the chap sitting right next to me in the shoulder.

We kept taking ammunition up to the front, and were supplying the tanks in particular. But they were horribly vulnerable. The Sherman tank that the British and Americans had was fast, but its armour and gun were very weak compared to the German Panthers and Tigers. I felt very sorry for the tank crews, because they had to take risks. I remember one field in Holland being covered in burning Shermans, all knocked out with just a single hole in them where they'd been shot.

That part of Holland is very low and flat, with lots of flooded areas. They have raised roadways to make sure they can still get about. Once an American plane came in to make an emergency landing on what he thought was a flat field, but the ground was very deceptive. He ended up going straight into the embankment of one of these roads, and the plane was smashed to pieces. Half of it just buried itself into the road. We saw a Spitfire crash too after a dogfight. The pilot must have been killed, because it came straight down vertically with its throttle wide open. The engine was making a hell of a noise, and it hit the ground about forty feet from me. It smashed into the earth and completely disappeared into a huge hole, not a bit of it was left above the ground.

We didn't get much time to ourselves, we were always busy. But we did try to get some extra food whenever we had the chance. I remember looking at a lagoon beside the river and saying to the boys, 'Look, I bet there's a lot of fish in there!' and we decided to go fishing. Rather than using a rod and line, or a net, I thought we could cause an explosion in the water to kill the fish and bring them to the surface. Of course I still hadn't learned my lesson about messing about in boats, and we went in search of a suitable craft to take us out. We found a load of little punts and rowing boats moored up just at the edge of the water. I managed to get hold of an anti-tank mine, which had a fuse which you could set to go off at a certain pressure. When it was buried in the ground, it was enough to blow up a Tiger tank. I set it to a light pressure, got into a punt with my mate, and rowed out into the middle of the lagoon. 'Right,' I said to him, 'when I drop the mine in the water, we'll only have a few seconds before it explodes. As soon as I drop it, you row like hell.'

He was ready, so I heaved it over the side and off he went. But he was rowing so hard that the rowlock, which holds the oar in place, snapped. He was panicking, and carried on rowing like mad with only one oar; which of course meant we went round in a circle! Now the '75 anti-tank mine is quite a piece of work, and *BOOM!* up it went up right under us. The bottom of the boat blew out, the rest of it fell to pieces, and I was left, once again, in the water with the remnants of my boat floating around me. We had to swim back to shore through loads of dead fish, and drip-dry our soaking battledress. All our mates were standing on the bank laughing their heads off.

Eventually Operation Market Garden fizzled out because our tanks didn't get to the paratroopers at Arnhem in time. We were so close, it was only a few miles from Elst, but the Germans took the bridge back and reinforced it. It meant that we couldn't do what Montgomery had wanted, and push on over the bridge into Germany, so we were withdrawn. It really had been a Bridge Too Far for us. We were set to have a chance to rest and recuperate.

We were quite close to the Rhine at one point, and I remember it most because of our stay at the cottage of a superintendent of the waterworks there. He had two very lovely daughters, and they came out to see us. They looked after us nicely and cooked us some fish. Willmore and I got lucky in the garden; he managed to sneak off with the older one and I had some fun with the younger one! I managed to impress her with some yellow parachute silk I'd pinched from one of the 'chutes which had come down near us during Market Garden a few weeks before. Unfortunately the grandfather, who was also living in the house, spotted us, and I got into trouble. The next time we went back to see them they wouldn't even open the gate!

Actually, we'd done quite well out of the supply drops in Market Garden, although not in the way they intended. As well as plenty of parachute silk, we'd gone scavenging in the gliders which had landed and been abandoned. We'd nicked the batteries inside them. They were very high quality ones, encased in metal instead of the usual fragile Bakelite. We put them in our trucks to make them more reliable.

We enjoyed a bit of rest, as our army regrouped. Despite the failure of Market Garden, everyone thought the war was being won. Nobody, not even Eisenhower, thought that the Germans had any real fight left in them. Then, at the coldest time of the year, when everyone was looking the other way, Hitler launched a massive counter-attack in the Ardennes. The Battle of the Bulge started, there was panic and confusion, and we were brought in to help fight off the last great German offensive of the war.

Chapter 10

THE BULGE

When the Allied leaders realised they wouldn't be able to capture the bridge at Arnhem, Operation Market Garden petered out. Instead of driving headlong towards Germany, we were pretty much told to stay put for a while. It gave us a chance to rest and get our supplies sorted out. The main attacks towards Germany were going on further south, and we were happy for them to get on with it! We were never far from Brussels and were able to get there every now and again.

It wasn't always safe though. We were in a village in Holland that was on the flight path of the V-1 flying bombs as they flew over to attack either the Allied armies or British cities. One night we were sleeping in this house and a flying bomb came over. We heard the motor cut out, and it came down in the village right next to us, landing in the local cemetery. The blast blew the roof off the house we were in and we were all left looking up at the stars!

But all of a sudden Hitler decided to catch everyone unawares. On 16 December he started this massive attack in the Ardennes, south-east from us. He wanted to come up and around us, capture the port of Antwerp, and encircle all of us in our army against the sea.

It particularly scared all the Americans who were in that area, because it was so unexpected. They started to retreat quickly, and for a while it looked as though the whole of the Allied front could collapse. Our commanders looked around for anyone who could come and help; and of course XXX Corps, including the Guards Armoured, was told to head for what was being called the Battle of the Bulge. It was called that because the Germans had made this big advance into our territory, in the shape of a bulge, and were heading north to try to get to the coast.

One area that Eisenhower and the others thought had to be protected was the Meuse river bridge near a place called Dinant; and that's where they sent us, as fast as we could go. We left on 20 December and drove as fast as we could towards the battle. If the Germans got as far as Dinant and managed to cross the river there, it would open up their advance and they could have caused the Allies real problems.

We got to Dinant last thing at night, and started digging holes straight away. We had nothing to do that with, apart from our basic entrenching tools. You always had to get down about two or three feet to make it properly safe, and you would try to drag something over the top of it to protect you. The ground was rock hard, and it took a lot of work to get down far enough.

Mind you, it was better than trying to dig in Holland. Six of us had dug a nice big trench there one night, and covered ourselves up in it with a tarpaulin. But the ground was so low that water began to seep in, and within a couple of hours we were all soaked.

The winter of 1944 was bitterly cold, especially around the Ardennes and the Meuse area. It started to snow, and it snowed all night. I remember waking up covered in snow and freezing cold. All you had to keep you warm was a groundsheet and a couple of blankets. We always slept in our holes when we were near the action, to get away from the lorries which were full of ammo. We didn't really know any details about what was going on, except that the Germans were coming and we had to help.

We knew the Germans were coming because the Americans told us.

We had seen lots of them on the way down, coming back in our direction. They warned us to stay away, 'Don't go down there!' they said. They looked terrible too; scared and scruffy. But we had to go to protect the bridge. Of course we were nervous because we didn't know when the attack might come. We loaded the tanks full of ammunition and off they went, ready to fight off any attack. We could hear the noise of the battle on the other side of the river, but they didn't get much closer. We just waited in our freezing foxholes and took ammo to the guns whenever they needed it. They would contact us by radio when they needed more supplies, and we'd jump in the lorries, load up with whatever was needed, and head out to them. In the end, the Germans got to within sight of us, just to the east, but were stopped. They had run out of fuel and supplies, and had been held up trying to capture the town of Bastogne because the Yanks refused to surrender even though they were surrounded. Then it was time for us to counter-attack, and we went across the river and pushed them out of a place called Celles on 27 December, just after Christmas Day. A few days later, as they retreated, we took Rochefort. That was the end of the battle for them; they retreated and we had done our bit in the Battle of the Bulge. I do remember being put in charge of dishing out the rum that Christmas Day. We were given several flagons of it and I had to make sure everyone had a fair amount every day, because it was so cold.

As their attack broke up and stopped, we were withdrawn again, towards Brussels to a village called Tirlemont where I used to help out serving tots of rum to the soldiers. It came to us in these big stone flagons, and it was just what you needed to warm you up a bit. There was a cafe there and the old girl who ran it used to make these lovely Belgian waffles. There wasn't much to the rest of the village, just a few houses and flats.

It was about this time that I managed to steal an American Jeep. The Yanks had abandoned it in their rush to get away, and I thought it might suit me very well. I think it had run out of fuel. There were always two of us in each truck who could drive, so I could be spared to pinch the Jeep.

The Passion Wagon!

Obviously I had mates who could supply us with petrol, so that Jeep became our passion wagon! I used to drive it over to Leuven, east of Brussels, with my mates in the back. Luckily all our vehicles had the same white star on them, so it could have belonged to anyone.

It wasn't all safe though. One night four of us decided to go to Leuven, and we set off in the dark. It was a moonlit night, and we were spotted by a German fighter. One of the boys spotted it, and shouted, 'There's a bloody plane coming down!' It came down and started firing at us, and I put my foot down and threw the jeep all over the road trying escape him. Luckily for us he gave up quickly and headed to the town. When we got to Leuven we could hear him shooting up other targets, and we jumped quickly into the first cafe we could find – where there were girls of course!

It was in Tirlemont that I met this old boy who asked me if I had any shotgun ammunition that I'd like to sell. At the time I didn't, but he made it clear that shotgun ammo was in really short supply. There were a lot of woods around there, full of animals to hunt, but the Germans had confiscated all the shotgun ammunition. I remembered that later on and made a nice few quid from it! Sadly I had to give the Jeep back after a few weeks.

We were then moved to a place near Maastricht and Aachen, called Sittard. It was there that I was attacked by a German jet fighter plane. It was daylight. Usually when you are bombed by aircraft you hear the engine noise first, so you have the chance to lie down or jump into some shelter. But this time there was no warning at all, just the scream of bombs. I threw myself flat, thinking, 'Where the hell are they coming from?' and a few moments later this jet came whizzing over our heads. It was very nerve-racking, because the Germans at this time were always showering us with propaganda leaflets. I remember one which said, *You've seen the V-1, and the V-2; what will be the next V-weapon?* and you didn't know what the hell to expect. It was very frightening. The pamphlets were designed to put the fear of God into us. And to be bombed by an aircraft you didn't even hear before it bombed you was scary. Luckily I'd learned by then just to get flat on the ground as fast as possible, and not to run around looking for shelter.

Every now and again we had to go into Maastricht to collect or drop things off. The road towards it was long and quite straight, and ran slightly downhill. I remember driving down it, going a good speed, when an American lorry overtook me and cut me up. I think it was part of the famous supply group called the Red Ball Express, which was run by black soldiers, because there were three black men in the front seat. Now I wasn't going to be overtaken, and I had a Ford V8 engine in my truck, so I put my foot down and absolutely hammered the engine for all it was worth. I got just about half way in front of them, and pulled quickly across to do to them what they'd done to me. They got pushed over onto the grass verge which had all these drainage ditches along it, and I saw them get bounced up and down as they drove over them! They tried to take me again, but there was no way I was going to let them. I did quite well, considering I had three tonnes of ammo in the back! They were quite a scary lot though, the Red Ball Express. Their job was just to keep the supplies coming as fast as possible from the beachhead or harbours, and to stop for nothing. We had to drive with our headlights reduced to little slits at night, and crawl along at fifteen miles an hour, to make sure we weren't attacked by the Jerries. You just had to follow the tail lights of the truck in front. But the Yanks always had their lights on full, and used to go roaring by us at fifty. They got us attacked several times by doing that. One of my mates got fed up with this, and mounted a big searchlight on the top of his truck. Sure enough, an American vehicle came along the road at full tilt towards us with all its lights on, so he switched on this searchlight and aimed it right at them. They ended up swerving off the road and into a tree!

Soon we started to move again, this time towards the Rhine and over into Germany. We went through Aachen, which had been smashed to pieces in the battle at the beginning of October. There was nothing left standing at all. It had been part of the Siegfried Line to defend the Fatherland, and was the first German city to be directly attacked. The Germans didn't want to give it up, and Hitler had ordered that it should be defended at all costs. As we drove through we could see the shattered remains of the deep defensive belt all around it. Our guns had fired into the city for six days, joined by bombing raids from aeroplanes to really knock the Germans out. But they had managed to stay in the ruins, and they had lots of bunkers too which hadn't really been affected by the bombing and shelling. The Americans had managed to fight their way through, and had even had to drive tanks and self-propelled guns up to bunkers and fire at point blank range to destroy them. By the time we got there, it was nothing but a heap of rubble.

Once we got past Aachen though, we had gone through the main German defences and it became a mad dash to get as far as possible into the Fatherland itself. There were abandoned positions and villages all over the place. I remember going through an abandoned airfield, which had obviously been bombed. There were wrecked German aircraft everywhere, and it was covered in shell holes which we had to drive around.

Hamburg was another place which had been really badly bombed, which we had to drive through later. The worst attacks had been back in 1943, when thousands of bombers attacked it for several nights running. Forty thousand people were killed there, and they carried on attacking it right up towards the end of the war because it had important oil refineries. It was just smashed to pieces. But really I had no sympathy for the Germans there, after what I'd been through, especially in London and Liverpool. We all thought it served them right; they'd done it to us, now we were doing it to them. I hated the German leaders for what they had done to so many people, but I don't think I ever really hated individual soldiers. They were stuck in it just like we were. What really amazed me in all the destroyed towns I saw was how fast they managed to make repairs. The women in particular got out into the streets and helped to shovel away the rubble and ruins to make the roads safe, and they got their services running very quickly again even as we drove through.

My brother Sid told me later of his lucky escape. He was in a different group to me, and was the last in a group of six ammo trucks heading to resupply troops attacking the Siegfried Line. He said he watched in amazement as every truck in front of him was hit, one after the other. *Bang, bang, bang,* and he jumped out of his truck just before it was blown up. He had to crawl back for more than a mile to get back to our lines. He thought it was an 88mm gun which had zeroed in on that bit of road to take out the supply columns.

Charlie was having a hard time too. He was in the relief column which took as much help as possible into the camp at Belsen, which had just been liberated. Everything we could spare was sent to the camp on our lorries. I asked him to tell me about it, but I couldn't get a word out of him. He just wouldn't talk about it at all, except to remember a huge pit filled with bodies. It wasn't until long afterwards that I found out about what he'd done. I don't think many of us really knew much about the camps at that point.

We were all quite relieved by then. I think we all knew that we were winning, and that we were getting towards the end of it. The Germans had been quite demoralised I think, by all the bombing and fighting, and also by the realisation that their country was being beaten. I remember stopping at one village and going up to a farm. A woman answered the door, and I asked '*Haben sie eier bitte?*' – 'Have you got any eggs'? And she said no, she didn't have any eggs. So I just lifted my Sten gun a little bit, and she said '*Ja, ja, wir haben eier!*' – yes she certainly did have some eggs! We were always careful though, and didn't just steal things – we always paid for eggs and other food, or gave them something in return. We didn't really fraternise much with the Germans though; we didn't want to mix with them. We'd had orders not to have anything to do with them anyway.

We were always on the lookout for food to supplement our rations. One time we were billeted in this big building which had a place where we could do some cooking. So I jumped into this Austin pickup truck with one of the cooks, and went out hunting. He was in the back with a .303 rifle. We came across this field full of geese all running around, and agreed that goose would make us a very nice meal that evening. He took careful aim, fired, and hit one of them. I jumped over the fence to go and grab it. But as I got hold of it, the other fifty geese were getting very agitated at having one of their friends shot. They started to chase me, hissing and flapping their wings as I tried to lug this twenty-pound bird back to the truck. I made it back to the fence and chucked it over, then managed to dive over myself before they got me! Of course my mate was laughing his head off.

I didn't have much better luck when I tried to get us a turkey. We were in this farm, and in the shed were three or four birds which we fancied for our dinner. I went in there and tried to catch one of them, but they were flapping all over the place and I couldn't do it. So I went into the house and grabbed a big carving knife. I went back to the shed and the turkeys were still running about. I waited until one came close enough to me and swung my knife. I managed to chop its head off. But the thing kept on running, without its head, and I had to carry on chasing it all over the place before it stopped. It did taste nice, though.

A lot of the places were just abandoned. We took over this mansion which had been owned by Heinrich Focke, one of the Focke-Wulf partnership which had designed German fighter planes. It was a lovely place, and as usual I went looking for cars. In the garage I found an Auto-Union racing car, and we pulled it out for a look. Because of my love of cars and racing I knew what it was; they had dominated motor racing before the war. Of course, I wanted to have a go in it, but its petrol tank was empty. We had some aviation fuel with us, which is much more potent than petrol, and poured that in. I got the boys to push me, but no matter how much we tried we couldn't get it to start. Regretfully we pushed it back into the garage and left it. There are hardly any of these wonderful cars left now. About fifteen years ago one of them was up for sale for six million pounds! It would have been a great passion wagon for me and the chaps.

The rest of the mansion was beautiful, like a palace. There was a ballroom, and other rooms with big plush carpets in. It hadn't been damaged by the war, and was beautifully preserved. I remember these clever cigarette lighters they had, which were plugged in to the wall. You had to tilt them over, the wick would be lit, and you would light your cigarette from that. It was very posh inside, and we would have loved to stay there for a while, but we were advancing so quickly we had to get on. We never took anything from there; in fact the only thing I came back from Germany with was a nice silver cutlery set from another house, which I gave to my mother.

Another time we took over a big posh restaurant. The cellar was full of champagne, vintage wines, brandy, everything nice. There was staff accommodation above the restaurant. We went up there to have a look around, to see if we could stay there that night. One of my mates noticed something strange about one of the lamp fittings. It was a sort of dish shape, which hung from chains beneath the light bulb. He put his hand in, and came out with a big diamond ring! 'I'll have that!' he said, and he did.

By this time, pushing through Germany, we weren't getting a terrific amount of resistance from the Germans, and we didn't have to dig holes every time we stopped any more. Instead, we'd look for little places we could grab as our own for a night or two. The Luftwaffe had all but given up by that point, and we became quite daring. We'd happily sleep above ground, without feeling vulnerable. Not all the Germans had given up though.

Once we stopped at this abandoned bungalow. We decided it would make an ideal spot for the night, and a friend of mine went in first. He headed to the toilet, before any of the rest of us could go. But when he pulled the chain it blew up, killing him outright. I was in the house at the time, and felt the explosion. We knew what had happened; we'd been warned about booby traps but perhaps we hadn't been careful enough about them. After my friend was killed, we used to check everything to make sure it wasn't connected to a wire or a pressure plate which could lead to a bomb. Door handles could be rigged to bombs, there could be tripwires; anything you touched could be rigged. We didn't get too upset though. It was part of life. After all I'd been through in the war, all the friends I'd lost and all the people I'd seen die, I just accepted his loss and moved on. That's what war does to you.

We became used to checking anywhere that we stayed at. One thing we did was to prod the garden of the bigger houses with a spike, to see if anything had been buried there, because they used to hide things. Once we were at a house where an old German and his family were still living. I took this spike and went over the garden, testing the ground. It went *squash, squash, squash, clink*! as I hit a metal box. We dug down and found a load of stuff which had been hidden, among which was a German Air Force officer's uniform. We went and got the man of the house, and asked if it was his uniform. 'Oh no,' he said, 'not mine.' So we made him put it on, and it fitted him perfectly! We pushed our guns into his back and handed him over to the infantry as a prisoner of war.

As the battles overtook the German army there were soldiers everywhere who didn't want to fight any more, just to survive and get back home. One day Willmore and I were walking though this wood at the back of a nice house. We wondered if there might be a pheasant or something we could eat. We came across this shed with a bird perched on top of it. I said, 'I bet you couldn't hit that bird!' and of course we both let fly with our Sten guns. We missed completely, but the door of the shed flew open and two young German soldiers came out with their hands on their heads! They wanted to surrender to us so we gave them a couple of cigarettes and handed them over to the infantry. It was virtually the only time I ever shot at a German soldier, accidentally or otherwise. I'm quite glad about that these days. I don't know if I could have lived with myself if I'd killed someone. It must be terrible, and I'm sure it must have given people nightmares. After all, they were only human beings anyway.

I have to say that the Red Cross at this time were amazing. They used to have little kiosks right up close to the Front, well in range of the guns, and they would give out tea and cakes for us. Often they were staffed by quite attractive young ladies, and that would give us a real boost as we tried to make ourselves brave!

We kept advancing, and we knew that it couldn't be much longer until the war was over. One day we had stopped at the side of the road – I don't know why – and General Montgomery turned up. We knew him as Monty. He pulled up in his big car, and told us all how well we were doing. He gave me a tin of two hundred cigarettes to share out. I was smoking quite a bit in those days, so they were a very welcome gift.

The Germans had been ordered to hand in every weapon to their local mayor, or *Burgomeister*. Shotguns, ladies' pistols, anything that could fire a bullet had to be given in; and all their cameras too. We were free to go there and take whatever we liked. So I came out with a Luger, a German pistol which everybody wanted, and a little .22 ladies' pistol, the sort of thing they could carry in a handbag. Lugers were popular because they were a mark of distinction, something which only certain people could get hold of. They also fired 9mm ammunition, which was quite handy. For a lot of the war the main British bullet size was .303, but in the lead up to D-Day a lot of new 9mm weapons were issued. That was great because the Germans used 9mm too, so if we seized an ammo dump there was a good chance that at least some of it would fit our guns. My Sten gun for example used it.

Much later, after the war was over, I was approached by a load of Yanks who wanted to buy my Luger. It was a real collector's item for them. We were in this yard which had a cobblestone floor. I was showing them the gun and pulled the trigger forgetting that I had a round in the breech, and of course it went off. The bullet smashed into the floor and ricocheted, whizzing past our heads with a hell of a noise and over the office where our major was. We all just scarpered as fast as possible, and I never completed the sale!

Everything was up for grabs really. We took over a German supply depot, and I managed to come into possession of a load of cases of Frappin which they had hidden away. There were twelve bottles in each case, marked *Deutsche Wehrmacht*. I went to headquarters and asked Captain King if I could have a truck and two men. He let me have them, and we went and loaded it up with the booze. When I came back the Captain couldn't believe it. I also managed to get hold of a half hundredweight sack of coffee beans, which were worth their weight in gold. I used to be able to use them to bargain for extra bread, cakes and other nice things, because everyone wanted coffee.

We also 'liberated' a big German generator. That came in very handy when we stayed in houses whose power had been cut off. We could plug the generator into the mains supply and have lights and everything switched on.

Another really unusual thing I found when I was digging about in this chateau was a big box full of Iron Crosses. There were loads of them in there, but none of them had been given out or had any engraving on them; they were just blank. We threw them into the rubbish, got rid of them, which is a shame because they'd probably be worth a fortune these days!

We were just enjoying these spoils of war when peace was declared. We were absolutely jubilant and went crazy, drinking the 'liberated' Frappin, and the whole company was drunk for several days. We'd been given a couple of tanks to protect the flanks of our advance, and I'd never driven one of those ... so we all decided we'd have a go, and one chap drove straight through a house! It was hard to get the hang of them, especially after lots of brandy, because you don't actually have a steering wheel. You have two levers which you pull or push to slow down individual tracks. Still, I'd driven nearly every other kind of vehicle on the Front, so it was nice to have a go on one.

I can't remember much else from that wonderful night, but I do remember waking up with my head in the toilet …

Chapter 11

GOING HOME

Once I'd retrieved my head from the toilet and straightened myself out, I realised that everyone else was in the same state as me. We didn't get much done that day, but we did have to get moving. I had a 1933 six-cylinder Mercedes saloon with swept mudguards, which I had nicked from somewhere in the village. I'd been driving that for fun alongside the column of trucks.

We set off towards our new destination, which was a place called Cuxhaven. We were to be part of the occupying forces. But it wasn't long before my lovely Mercedes got a puncture, and I had to stop to fix it while the convoy moved on. I think my friends in the trucks must have just laughed and driven on, but I managed to change the wheel and get moving again. A few miles further down the road, and I had another flat tyre! The tyres on the car had no tread left on them; I don't think they had been changed for a long time.

The column was long gone, and I was alone, on a deserted road, in the middle of what still felt like enemy territory. I walked on for about half a mile when I saw a German army camp. It was a motor pool, where they held all sorts of cars and vehicles. I had my Sten gun cocked under one arm, and my other hand was on the Luger pistol in my back pocket.

I walked on up the drive with my heart in my mouth. I was worried that even though the war was over they could still have knocked me off if they wanted to. There was a German officer at the top of the drive, with about a dozen uniformed men gathered around him. I pointed my Sten gun at him, and as I approached he came to attention, and called all his men to do the same. Luckily, he spoke very good English. He asked me what they could do for me. I told him I had a Mercedes with two flat tyres, and asked if he had a similar car whose tyres I could pinch. He said, 'No, but please take your pick of any of the other vehicles.' There were a lot of them parked across the camp. I saw one I liked, a French model with the gear stick in the dashboard.

'I'll have that one.' I said.

'Sorry, you can't have it,' he replied, 'It hasn't got any petrol in it.'

I took a look around. 'Has that other one got any in the tank?' I asked.

'Yes.' he said.

I took a firm grip on my pistol. 'Then get someone to siphon the petrol out of it and into that French car!'

I must have looked mean because he got one of his men to do it right away! When they'd finished siphoning petrol into the car I wanted I jumped in, drove off, and finally managed to catch my convoy. I could recognise my group from its identification sign, the all-seeing eye. It was on all the vehicles.

I managed to keep that car for a few days before the officers made me hand it in.

We carried on in convoy to Cuxhaven. One incident I remember clearly from there involved a group of German sailors. A lot of the *Kreigsmarine*, or German Navy, still considered themselves Nazis, and they hated us. These sailors were walking towards me and my mates on the pavement, and it was clear as we got closer and closer that they weren't going to step aside for us. As we got right up to them we raised our guns, making an obvious threat, and even though they didn't like it, they had to back down and step into the road. After all, we were the winning army; we had fought for years to defeat them and their Nazi leaders. We had to show them who was boss.

We didn't get much trouble other than that though, because I think the Germans knew that they were beaten. Most of them, like us, were just relieved that it was all over.

We were moved back down to a place called Wahn, outside Cologne. My situation changed there, after the man who ran the officers' mess was sent home. In civvy life Bert was the head waiter at the Ritz Hotel, and I was asked to take over his job in the mess. He taught me all the nonsense of how to run it, and I became quite good at it. I had to go and buy all the supplies of food and drink, and whatever other little 'extras' I could find!

To Mum and All at Home with Love from Bill

Cologne, 17. Sept. 1945

I had a good relationship with my officer, Captain King, and he and I used to go to Brussels regularly to stock up. The area around our camp at Wahn was still lined with German bunkers, and we used to go in them to

114

see what we could find. One of them was full of shotgun ammunition, and I remembered the man in Tirlemont who'd asked me if I could find some a few months before, during the Battle of the Bulge. I realised it must be quite a valuable commodity, so I made contact with him again. We'd pick up a few cases of ammo from the bunker each trip and sell it on to him. We used the money to buy lots of brandy and all sorts of other goodies for the mess. Captain King was a good, friendly officer who'd been an insurance man in civvy street, and we got quite good at making some dodgy deals. We drove about in a V8 gun truck, and often went through Aachen. MPs would stop us at checkpoints there, to see our papers and ask what we were up to. But luckily they never asked to look in the back!

The mess was called the Eye Club. That's because the Guards Armoured Division sign was the all-seeing eye, and we were quite proud of it. I'd drop him off there, then head on to stay at the home of other friends we had made in the area. It meant that I could keep hold of the truck for a few days too, as transport for my mates! We often used it to go on hunting expeditions to supplement our rations. I'd take my shotgun, plus as much ammunition as I wanted from our special bunker, and see what we could find. There were a lot of pheasants about, and once I brought back five or six to the mess. A major there told me to 'hang them until their heads drop off.' So I did. And I wished I hadn't. They stank, and they tasted exactly the same as they smelled!

The chef at the mess was German, and I became quite friendly with him. He had a young daughter, and I used to take some beer and food to his house for a meal and a drink.

The only problem we had was that down the road there was an old German barracks, which still held about fifteen thousand Russians. I think they had volunteered to work for the Germans. The authorities must have been waiting to find out what to do with them. They kept escaping, and roaming around our area raping and looting. I remember going down this road with a row of houses down one side, and a woman came out yelling and screaming. Two Russians had been in her house, so we went in and threw them out. We chased them off, but as they got further down the road they turned as if to come back. We got our guns and fired a burst over their heads, and they scarpered properly this time.

It was a time when lots of people across Europe were trying to either find their way home, or find someone to help them. There was one woman who was always hanging around outside the mess, trying to pick up a soldier to be her boyfriend. The problem was, she wouldn't go with any old soldier, she wanted to get herself an officer – but none of them wanted to know!

I got the worst wound of my war at the chateau in Wahn. I was standing at a window when I saw a rat running across the yard. I thought, 'I'll have that ruddy thing!', and I picked something up and threw it at the rat. But as I did so I caught my fingernail on the window frame, and tore it. The shock of it made me faint! It reminded me of a similar incident when I was a kid learning the fish trade. I was using a knife, and sliced my finger by the nail; again, I fainted right out!

Eventually my brothers and I got leave to go back to Jersey, which had only recently been liberated. Of course it's a complicated journey to get back to Jersey, and the travelling ate into our leave. So we went to the Grand Hotel, which had been a German headquarters but had now been taken over by the British. We told them our mother wasn't very well, and some other sob stories, and they let us stay for longer.

It was very strange coming back to our little island. Remember, I had been away in London, Liverpool, and half of Europe before I went home. I remember very clearly going up Conway Street in St Helier, then turning into New Cut, and thinking, 'Oh my God, I didn't realise it was so SMALL!' The roads were tiny. But first things first – my brothers gave me some money, and said, 'Go and buy a motor car.' So I headed down to the cattle market in Minden Place, which in those days used to sell cars on a Saturday afternoon. It's now a car park, but then you could get almost anything you wanted there. I put a bid in on a DeSoto, which must have been built in about 1928. It had wooden wheels, and when I drove it around a corner they used to go *clackety clack, clackety clack*! I filled it up with petrol and we drove it out to Ouaisne, which is only about five miles away, but on the way back it ran out!

I parked it up at my brother's house on Bagot Avenue. But then the son of old Mr Mourant the farmer came up behind me with a tractor and insisted that I move. I got the starting handle out and cranked it over; and it started. But the handle was stuck in the socket, and as the engine kept running the handle kept flying around and almost destroyed the radiator. I was really mad at him, and told him I could have driven a tank past my car, let alone a tractor! But it wasn't the best car; the window fell out when I slammed the door.

It was wonderful to be back with all my family for that short time, even though the Germans had made a mess of the island while I'd been away. There were huge bunkers everywhere. One on Conway Street in town was so big that it took three months to demolish it. People were still using the German Occupation money too, because they hadn't been able to organise an alternative yet. In the last few months of the war they'd been starving, because no supplies could get through. Trees had been cut down, and people had burned their furniture, just to get a fire going to keep warm. I felt proud that I had done my bit to end the war, and get the Germans out of my island. I'd even volunteered to be part of a force to liberate the island, by parachuting onto it. But that plan had never really come to anything, and looking at all the defences I'm quite glad about it; I don't think any attack would have done anything except cause lots of death and damage. It would have devastated the population.

Our leave was all too short though, and we were all soon back on duty in Wahn. While it wasn't too hard, I just couldn't get home fast enough. Men were getting discharged after finishing their time, and I wanted to be one of them. Luckily, when I'd signed up I'd described myself as a plasterer/

builder. The reason that was lucky is that after the war anyone involved in the construction trade was released early because of the destruction in England. So I finally got my release. I was still working at the mess in Wahn when my papers came through, and the officers pleaded with me to stay. I think they enjoyed all the little extras I was getting them. But I said no way, I was going home as fast as I could!

I was demobbed shortly before Christmas 1945. I made my way to Ostend to catch the ferry to England. There were loads of soldiers on board, all happy like me to have survived the war and to be going home. I had my kitbag full of gear with me, including the Luger and the ladies' pistol which I had liberated from the Germans. But as we approached England, there were tannoy announcements telling us that we weren't allowed to keep any weapons or ammunition with us. So, very sadly, the Luger and the little pistol went over the side. When we got to the port, there were rows of military policemen who stopped random soldiers and asked them to turn out their bags, but they didn't stop me! So I missed out on the guns, but I did manage to bring back a set of silver knives, forks and spoons which I had found in a German house. I gave them to my mother.

Before I left France I remember buying a big chicken to take home to the family for a nice meal. I'd also managed to get away with a bottle of the naval rum which I'd been dishing out to the soldiers, so we could have a great time. There was myself, my sister and brother-in-law, and their daughter for Christmas. They were living in one of the newly built prefab homes that were being built all over the country, because their flat had been blown apart by the Germans. We had quite a few noggins of the rum, and were well under by the end of the evening.

The next day I had to catch the train to the demob centre. I got on, still feeling the worse for wear, and managed to fall asleep and miss my station. I ended up down in St Austell, and had to change trains and come all the way back up again overnight. At the demob centre they gave me my pay and a demob suit which wasn't very nice and didn't fit me; I never wore it.

It did come in useful though. When I finally got back to Jersey, I went to a tailor I knew and asked him to make me a suit. The problem was, you had to have coupons for clothes then, and I didn't have enough. 'Don't worry,' the tailor said, 'Give me your demob suit. I know a French man who will buy it, and you can use those coupons.' So that's what I did, and I got a nice suit made up especially for me.

We were allowed to keep the army clothes we stood up in; I don't think they wanted loads of second-hand battle dress. So I turned up in everything I had, including my nice heavy greatcoat and army boots. I kept it all to go to work in, and the coat in particular was very useful when it was cold. It was wool though, and didn't half hold the water! It was the stuff that had got me through the war, and I was relieved to have come through it when so many other people had been killed or wounded. But now it was time to get my life back on track, and start earning some money. Some of my family had been in the island right through the Occupation, so it was easy to get back into the swing of things.

My brother George had decided to stay during the war to look after his family and the business. Amongst other things, he'd converted an old copper into a still and made loads of Calvados, which he sold. He told me it was a very lucrative enterprise! But he'd also done some work for the Germans. In 1942, Hitler had ruled that anyone who wasn't born in Jersey should be deported to camps in Germany, and hundreds were sent off to Bad Wurzach and other places. Of course we had all been born in London. But they struck a deal with George. They were having problems getting enough workers to build new roads, because no one wanted to work for them. They told George that if he used his three company vans and some reliable workers to help them, they wouldn't deport him and his family. He had a three-year-old daughter and a little baby, and he couldn't face the idea of them being sent away. So he agreed to help the Organisation Todt, which was responsible for all the German roads, bunkers and emplacements. His job was to go down to the docks with the vans, load up supplies and take them to where the work was being done. But he was sneaky too. When the guards weren't looking, he'd go up to any vehicle which had been commandeered, lift up the bonnet, and whip out the rotor arm from the engine. Of course they couldn't run without those, and he'd chuck them quietly into the water of the harbour.

On one occasion he managed to 'liberate' a huge tin of treacle from the German supplies at the docks. He lifted up the bonnet of his truck and hid it in the engine. But of course the roads at that time were very bumpy and pot-holed, and as he drove away the tin got a hole in it. All the way from the harbour up to the supply depot, he said, there was a trail of sticky treacle on the road following him!

Another time he nicked a load of petrol from the German supplies and drove it back to his bungalow on Queen's Road. But as he was putting it in the garage, his wife saw a German officer coming through the front gate. 'Quick!' she said, 'If you've got anything to get rid of, do it right away!' So while she kept the officer talking, he moved the cans of petrol into another vehicle. The officer came through to the garage, and felt the engines of the trucks there, to see which one had just been used. When he got to the one George had just come in with, he searched right through it, but didn't find anything. That was a very lucky escape, because stealing petrol was a serious offence. I think George did exactly the right thing really, in agreeing to stay and work; you couldn't say no to the Germans because they could just put you up against a wall and shoot you. A lot of Jersey people had been very brave in that way.

Not everyone understood though. I remember clearly going to one family home in St Peter on my rounds with the van very soon after I got back. The woman opened the door and saw our family name on the van. 'Get out, get out!' she said, 'I'm not buying anything from someone who worked for the Germans!' So I opened up the white coat I was wearing and showed her my battledress, the one I'd worn all the way through France, Belgium, Holland and Germany. 'Does it look like I worked for the

Germans, Madam?' I asked. I got back into the van and drove off.

Not many people seemed to want to know about what I'd done in the war. There was a mood in the island that they had been through a terrible time, and they wanted to put it behind them. Nobody cared about what people like me, or other returning soldiers, had done. Apart from my family, no one asked me anything about it, no one made a fuss, you were just expected to get on. But to be honest, I didn't want to tell them anyway. I'd been through some terrible things and I didn't want to go through it all again. I just wanted to be home, and to enjoy myself living a normal, safe life. I didn't even talk about it with my brothers who I had served with; we just kept quiet about it. I loved having the freedom of civilian life, no one shouting or shooting at you, no parades, and sleeping in my own bed. Home-cooked food was such a luxury too, after years of army rations. I couldn't forget the war quickly enough, to be honest.

I was lucky that George had managed to keep a fish delivery business going during the Occupation. I started work with my brothers, and was paid more than I would have got elsewhere. I had to work for a year to learn the trade, and then I would become a partner. One of the first things I had to do was get some vehicles for us. Ours had been requisitioned by the Germans early in the war, and they'd all been collected together afterwards at Springfield Stadium in town. So I went down there and found the three family Commer vans dating back to 1940. I tried them out, but found that only one of them was really serviceable. I bought it, and it was my vehicle until I got a new Austin Ten van later. We arranged them so that when you opened the back doors it looked like a little fish shop, with everything nicely laid out for the customers.

We did quite well because we worked hard, and eventually we had a fleet of seven vans which we took all over the island. One was kept as a spare, and one was just for deliveries to hotels and guest houses, which were starting to get busy again after the war.

Fish was actually quite a good business to be in, because during the

Occupation people hadn't been able to go to sea and go fishing. It meant that there were loads of fish to be taken, and we were able to get top quality stock. We even bought a boat, the *Fiona*, and paid a man to work it for us, bringing in shellfish, lobsters and crabs. To keep up with demand, we bought fish from Grimsby too, and shifted tons every week.

I never actually liked the job very much though; it was very hard work. I'd start at six in the morning, wrapped up in my greatcoat, and go to the fish market to where all the stock was stored. I'd load my van up with boxes of fish then go home for some breakfast. Just after eight, I'd start my rounds, delivering to houses all over the place. I was usually done by about half past five, when I'd have to come back and clean the van ready for another day. On a Saturday I had to do the lobster orders, and all the hotels in those days used to like to give their customers lobster. Some days I would deliver more than a tonne of them, in relays across the island.

I worked for a year to earn a partnership in the business, and earned some good money. But driving around delivering fish wasn't enough for me. After all the excitement of driving during the war, all the trucks, tanks, DUKWs and cars, I knew what I wanted to do. I loved speed, I loved the thrill of danger, and I'd grown up watching the sand races and hill climbs around Jersey. I wanted to race.

Part 12

RACER

I bought my very first racing car in 1947 from a man called Alex who ran a shop in Stopford Road. It was an Austin Seven, and I'm sure I paid too much for it. But I loved it – it would do about seventy-eight miles an hour flat out. I remember hammering it along the Five Mile Road, which runs

Getting ready to race on St Ouen's beach

My Taylor Special. Notice the six-foot exhaust pipe and the fuel tank right behind my seat.

next to the beach on the west cost of the island. It was quite frightening actually, because the road was in pretty poor shape after the war, and I was bounced around all over the place.

I wanted to go faster though, so I went to see a friend of mine called Harold Taylor, who was an engineer and belonged to the racing club. He had the plans for a new car based on a 1000cc motorbike engine, which he had been going to build for a customer who had recently died. He asked me if I wanted the car instead, and I said yes. It was a real custom-built machine, designed around me. It was very fast, especially after we changed the engine and the compression ratio. We ran it on a fuel mixture we called dope, and it went like a rocket. I can't remember the exact formula, but dope was a concoction of benzene and ether. It was expensive stuff, about seven pounds a gallon, where petrol was just half a crown.

We called the car the Taylor Special. It was small, with an open cockpit, and had no protection for the driver at all really. It was just an engine

*Bouley Bay hill
climb at the
start line*

Bouley Bay, Les Platons corner

bolted to the side of a simple chassis right next to the driver, with a big steering wheel. We used the seat and a few other bits from an old Fiat 500 to finish it off. It didn't have a seat belt because they didn't really exist in those days. On the front it had proper wishbone suspension, controlled by shock absorbers. At the back it had a solid axle, with a sprocket on it which took the drive from the engine through a chain. The axle was held above the chassis, to keep everything low, and had suspension based on a piece of glider tow rope. You could adjust the suspension for different races just by changing the rope. I proudly painted the fuel tank myself, and it looked lovely. But the first time I filled it up the dope ran over the paintwork and stripped it right off! The rest of the car was painted silver, or just bare aluminium. I gave my old Austin to my brother-in-law, who raced it on the beaches. But I think he ran it without oil, and he wrecked the engine.

There were so many races to do in Jersey, and it was a really popular pastime. There were hill climbs up Bouley Bay, where you'd race against the clock, and sprints along Five Mile Road which were timed too. But the most exciting was sand racing, where loads of you would fly around a circuit on the beach. It gave my car a hard time though, and we had to make all sorts of modifications to keep it going.

One problem was that the engine of the Taylor Special was bolted directly onto the chassis. All the vibrations from driving over rough roads and beaches loosened the bolts, and bits used to drop off! During one race I was getting very close to the finish when I noticed I was losing power. I checked the engine, and saw that one of the carburettors was coming away. So I held it on, and drove the rest of the way with one hand on the carburettor and one hand on the steering wheel! I wanted to get the problem sorted out, so I took her to a friend of mine called Ron Jimson, who knew lots about cars. He drilled a hole through every bolt, and put split pins through them so they wouldn't come loose. I kept losing the mudguards we'd made to stop the sand hitting me because of the same problem, so we fixed those too.

I started to do quite well in the races because I was brave, took risks, and pushed the car hard. I remember one hill climb at Bouley Bay, when I was just a second and a half down on the leader after my first run. I thought, 'I can do better than that!' and decided to change my tactics a little bit. Instead of taking off in second gear, I started in first and really floored it. When I got to a bend called Radio Corner, the time-keepers were amazed, they said I was ten seconds faster than anyone! But I hit the brakes too hard because I was going too fast, and the next thing I knew I was up the bank and off the course. I pulled myself together, got the car going again, and got back onto the road. Despite my unscheduled pit stop, I finished in sixty seconds dead; just two seconds slower than my first effort. Later I took a razor blade to my back tyres and made lots of little slits in them. As I went faster, they would open up a little and give me more grip.

On another occasion there I was determined to keep my foot down all the way through the finish line. The problem was that the road was concrete, and had lots of cracks running across it. By the time I got to the line, the back of the car was overtaking the front, and I spun completely round after I crossed the line.

But the most memorable race was on the beach at St Ouen. The island has big tides, and you get a massive area of beach exposed when the water goes out. It was what we called a fifty miler, where we had to go around a one-mile circuit fifty times. I needed to prepare carefully for it, because it was held on a Thursday afternoon and I had to make sure my work was done. So I spoke to my customers, and they agreed that I could do their Thursday deliveries on Wednesday evening. That meant a very long Wednesday for me; I did a full round, came back to the shop to load up again, and went out with fresh supplies to everyone. I finished at about nine in the evening. I still had to do some work in the morning, but much less, and sometimes my brother used to help me. I got back to the market at about midday, unloaded, cleaned the van, and got ready to race. The car was all prepared, so all I needed to do was nip home to change. I had a set

of brown padded RAF flying overalls which gave me a bit of protection. I collected the car from Ron Jimson at the garage, and towed it down to the beach. I had to get there by half past two. There was already a great atmosphere there, with crowds of people waiting to watch us race. It was early closing day, so lots of locals were there, as well as hundreds of tourists. I knew everyone who was racing, and we were all very friendly.

The course was set out already, with markers in the sand showing which way we had to go. The course was roughly oval, with long straights and smooth corners. In the pit area, everyone was milling around, chatting, getting cars ready, and making last-minute adjustments. I remember the smell of dope and Castrol R racing oil as we topped up and made sure everything was right for racing. The atmosphere was wonderful, really special, and we were all excited.

We lined up, about twenty of us in all different types of cars, the marshal dropped the flag and off we went, sand flying everywhere as we tried to get in front for a clear run. I accelerated carefully to start with, because if I just floored it from a standstill the back would overtake the front. Everyone wanted to get into the lead, because you could see what you were doing. Some of the bigger cars like the Ford V8s were using town and country tyres, which had great big treads like army vehicles. If you got stuck behind one of those they would throw great big chunks of sand and rocks at you. I had a visor on my helmet, and mudguards, but even so the stuff got absolutely everywhere. I did well, and managed to get into the lead. I was hitting a hundred miles an hour along the straights, and managed to keep it fast through the corners too. On the chicane I would get very close to the barrels which marked the course out, lift my foot a little to let the car right itself, then go flat out to the floor again. It felt so fast, because the car was so low I was practically sitting on the floor, and the engine right beside me was screaming away. The seat was just bolted to the chassis, so I got bumped around and thrown about a lot. As I drove I had to keep checking the petrol tank, which was also beside me. It was pressurised, to push the fuel into the carburettors. That meant I had to pump it up by hand every now and again, even while I was racing flat out. I was in the lead, but that's when my problems started.

The first thing to go was my brakes. I put my foot to the floor but nothing happened. The vibration from the engine had broken the hydraulic pipe leading to the calipers. I managed to swerve into the pits, but Ron said, 'Sorry, there's nothing I can do.' So I had to get back out there and race with no brakes. I went out, and went just as fast as I had been going before, a hundred along the straights, and then dropping down the gears to slow me down for the corners. The compression ratio on the engine meant that if you dropped it down into third at that speed it worked like a brake and you could just about get round the corner without losing too much speed. It worked, and by forty-six miles I was four laps ahead of anyone else.

Then I lost the clutch. The nipple on the end of the cable, which held it in place, broke off and the cable just pulled through.

With just a couple of laps to go I had to push on as well as I could. I'd practiced changing gear without the clutch in the delivery vans, just listening to the sound of the engine, and now I did the same, trying to get to the finish as quickly as I could. But there was one more accident waiting to happen. I flew into a corner very fast, and hit one of the ruts which had built up during the race. The impact threw the engine's driving chain off the sprocket, and it fell between the sprocket and the gearbox housing. I managed to get to the pits, but we couldn't fix it; the thing was jammed. If it had come off the other side it would've been easy to fix. We had to take the whole gearbox apart to free it, by which time the race was over and somebody else had won. It was very frustrating, because I had always wanted to win a fifty-miler, but really exciting too.

Of course racing like that could be dangerous, although I never really got hurt. But I remember one race where I'd been taking it easy because I was running in a new set of bearings. I watched a friend of mine called Sid racing around in his 'blown' Austin Seven. 'Blown' meant that it had been fitted with a supercharger to make it much faster. Towards the end of the race I thought my bearings were probably OK, so I opened up the engine and went flying off. I came to a corner and started to cruise around it, a bit more slowly. As I turned I could see Sid flying into the bend, coming at me much too fast, and I remember saying, 'Take your bloody foot off, you're going to turn!' No sooner had I said it than he turned over and bounced: from the wheels over onto his head, to the wheels, onto his head. He was rushed to hospital and was in a coma for about three months. When he woke up he didn't recognise anyone. I went to see him with a friend called Bill. When we got to his bed I said, 'Hi Sid!' and he said, 'Who's that?'

'Bill Reynolds.'

'Ah,' he said, 'The Taylor Special!'

That had been the last car in his mind, and the memory sort of brought him back a little. He was never the same man again though, his brain had been damaged. It was very sad; he'd been a top racer and owned a garage.

But that accident never put me off racing, and I kept trying to go faster and faster. I bought a works MG, which looked like a Maserati, for a hundred pounds. It was nice, but nowhere near as fast or exciting as my Taylor Special. I ended up raffling it for a hundred pounds to get rid of it. A few years ago one went up for auction in London, and it went for a hundred and seventy-five thousand pounds!

I went on to kart racing after that, and had a Villiers 197, one of the fastest you could buy. In those days we raced up at Quennevais, and it was quite fast and furious. In one race I was coming into a bend against another boy, and neither of us was going to back down. But he played a dirty trick on me, one which we would never have done in sand racing. He flipped the back of his kart onto the front of mine, which pushed me up onto the bank.

Over the years I won quite a few prizes and cups, and really enjoyed it. But then I came close to being killed; not when I was racing but while I was spectating.

It was the Jersey International Road Race of 1949. Every year they'd

close The Avenue, the main road along the coast from St Helier, and all
the fastest cars would race along there, past Bel Royal, and back again. I'd
worked all day, because practice for the event would happen in the evening.
It was a beautiful day, and there were crowds of people ready to watch.
At that time, just a few years after the Occupation, people wanted to see
something exciting. Motor sport had a huge following then in the island.

I wasn't going to be racing. My car wasn't qualified to international
standards because it didn't have a reverse gear or a handbrake, and because
of its unusual custom build. I'd volunteered to be a marshal, so that I could
be a part of the whole event. I dressed smartly, including a brand new pair
of brown shoes.

The place I had to supervise was at a difficult part of the course. As you
get to the end of The Avenue, at Bel Royal, the road bends quite quickly
to the right, and then back off to the the left again. It's quite a chicane, and
Bel Royal Motors is just on the corner there. We set up barriers to keep the
crowd off the road, and together with a police sergeant and a doctor had
it all under control. One of the barriers cordoned off the escape road, for
cars which overshot the bend and needed to go straight on; that got quite
crowded with people.

The practice session was going really well, and there were some really
good drivers throwing their cars around that corner extremely fast. They
all wanted to set the fastest time. The crowd loved it, and it was all very
exciting to see them so close up on a normal road.

But then a Bugatti came around the first part of the turn faster than
anyone, and I knew something was wrong. He'd lost his brakes; the cables
were trailing under the car making sparks as they dragged along the
road. I don't think he realised it until he put his foot on the pedal and
nothing happened. He was heading straight for the escape road at about
eighty miles an hour, but he saw that it was full of people who could get
hurt. I saw him pull the wheel over to try to head on the road up towards
Beaumont instead, a last moment decision. At that speed though, his tyres

just wouldn't take it. He was coming straight at us. I started to run, but it was too late. He broadsided straight into us.

(Courtesy Jersey Evening Post)

He hit me with the front wheel from behind as he bounced over the kerb. I was flung back across the bonnet, which smashed all the ribs on my left side. The impact threw me nearly twenty feet up in the air, and I can clearly remember looking down and seeing all the debris flying about below me. One of my brand new shoes was flung off. Then of course I came crashing back down to the ground, and started having convulsions as my body tried to get some air back into my lungs. I remember shaking uncontrollably and the chaos going on around me, but I couldn't do a thing about it. I passed out. I was really lucky because one of the first aid attendants was just around the corner behind the barrier. Later he told me that he'd almost fallen over me as he came rushing across, and then given me emergency treatment right away.

I was unconscious when they put me into the ambulance, but I remember waking up and shouting, 'I'm not going to die! I'm not going to die!' as they drove me to the hospital. I could hear another person moaning. That was the Bugatti driver, and I found out later he died in the ambulance next to me. The police sergeant and the doctor who I had been chatting to just moments before had been thrown over the wall and smashed up very badly; they both died almost immediately.

I was the only survivor of the accident, thanks to the medics who worked on me at the scene, in the ambulance and at the hospital. They literally brought me back. As well as my ribs, my hip bones were all chipped, but hadn't broken. For months afterwards, pieces of bone kept pushing through the skin around the tops of my legs. I was on crutches for three months. Some time later I went back to the hospital because my foot hurt badly, and I knew something wasn't right. They put me under gas to knock me out a bit, and started to manipulate it. Even though they were giving me gas, I shouted so hard, with some very choice words, that they knew I must have broken some bones. They should really have X-rayed it properly before.

I must have been pretty tough though, because other than that I got away with it. It left a beautiful imprint of a tyre on the back of my leg for a long time. I was very lucky to have escaped, and also very lucky to have had my wartime experience to draw upon. I had seen death, and terrible injuries, close up, and lost some of my friends, so I was able to cope better than other people might have. Mind you, as a smoker who needed to cough all the time, the broken ribs were a real pain.

The news of the crash got out very fast of course, but some people got the wrong end of the stick from the papers. My brother was on a round out in St Ouen, delivering fish, when a woman said to him "So sorry to hear about your brother."

'What do you mean?' he asked. 'Well he's dead, in a car crash,' she told him, 'I read it in the paper.'

What had happened was that the paper had published the names of people who had been hurt or killed and she thought I had been one of the victims. If those medical people hadn't been so good, she might have been right.

'A man called Kingsley Pipon had nearly bought it too. He'd been sitting on the wall with his two sons when he saw the car coming at him. He'd pushed the boys backwards over the wall to save them, but hadn't quite been quick enough himself. The car crushed his foot as it bounced up over the pavement. He ended up in the same hospital ward as me, and we became good friends. The discipline in the ward was very strict. An Irish sister enforced a strict curfew, lights out and no talking after nine o'clock in the evening. At six in the morning you'd be given a bowl of water to shave in, and then they would bring you breakfast. The problem was, I had loads of friends who came to see me, my brothers and all the racing lads, and they all brought me grapes to eat. I had so many I didn't know what to do with them, so in the end we had a grape fight! It helped to lighten the atmosphere. The Sister came in while we were in the middle of it, and she was far from impressed!

As well as the scars, the accident left me with a real fear of being next to a racing car. I raced again myself, but for a long time I got really nervous of someone else revving an engine near me. What eventually cured me was working as a flag marshal at the following year's race. There were no accidents, and I was hooked again. I couldn't stay away from fast cars. The only thing that would stop me racing was love.

Chapter 13

FALLING IN LOVE

It was while I was on two sticks that I met her. My friends and I used to enjoy a drink and the odd game of cards, and one of the chaps I used to play with was Oscar Horman, who used to like the racing too.

One evening he said, 'Come on, let's go back to my place and have a game of poker.' So we headed off in the car, and got back to his house. It was a lovely place on Victoria Street, a listed granite building with turrets and railings which looked beautiful. He'd forgotten his keys, so we had to knock on the door. It was answered by his sister Doreen, and that was it for me. It was the first time I'd seen her, and it was love at first sight. We sat down and I can remember the two of us just looking at each other. We didn't really even speak. She was still in her dressing gown, because the family was just going off to bed.

A few days later I chatted to her other brother, who was giving her driving lessons at the time, in a lovely old two-litre Jaguar. He let me know where I might conveniently run into them, for example they often went to the Britannia pub at Bel Royal after a lesson. The problem was that I couldn't drive because of the accident, so I had to get someone else to take me around. Bill Farnham drove my Vanguard, and became my chauffeur. We used to follow Doreen's Jag as she had her driving lessons, to see where she went! She cottoned on though, and asked her brother 'Who's that car following us?'

But it gave me a way to meet her, and we finally got chatting. I asked her out on a date, she accepted ... and three months later we were engaged. We used to go to the West Park Pavilion, the 'Pav', which was THE place to meet people. We'd dress up nicely and go dancing there, often to Doug Tanguy and his band. I'd been out with a lot of girls before, but never found the right one. One evening I simply asked her, 'Will you marry me?' I'm so lucky she said yes.

It wasn't all plain sailing though. Her father wasn't really sure of me, so he asked one of her brothers to investigate me. He didn't want his daughter to marry just anyone, he wanted someone who would treat her well. He was a wealthy man. When the results came in, I was approved of.

In those days your stag night was always held the night before your wedding, and of course lots of my friends took me out for a 'good time'. When morning finally came, on 19 June 1950, I was really the worse for wear. I got up at about six in the morning and drove around for two or three hours with my head out of the window trying to blow the cobwebs away! By the time I got home my family were all up and about, dressed and drinking champagne. I managed to get myself upstairs and started to put on my hired morning suit. But I hadn't checked the trousers properly and they were about six inches too long! My mother had to do a quick sewing and ironing job to make me look presentable.

The wedding went beautifully though. It was at the Town Church, right in the centre of St Helier. My brother Charlie was my best man. Lots of Doreen's relations came over from France; a part of her family is French.

I never touched a drink that day; after the night before I just couldn't.

The honeymoon was a real adventure. We were going on a driving holiday, all over Europe, as if I hadn't had enough of that during the

139

A romantic start to our honeymoon

war! But getting there was nearly as complicated as D-Day. We flew over to Dinard because the car was being taken on a freight boat over to St Malo. There wasn't a proper ferry then, and we used the British Railways boat the *Brittany*.

When we got to the hotel there was a huge storm going on. A burst of fork lightning came down and hit the tree just outside our room. What a great start to a marriage! The next morning we took the ferry back to St Malo to pick up the car. We went to the docks to watch them take it out of the hold of the boat. They used a huge crane to lift it, and then swung it over the side and onto the quay. As they did it, I heard one of the dockers shout '*Ouf, regarde, les harengs fumés!*' Smoked kippers - and there were a load of them all tied with wire to our exhaust pipe! My brothers had sneakily taken the car to the garage the day before, rolled it over the inspection pit, and sabotaged it. Everyone was pointing, clapping and laughing. As they lowered my car onto the ground, one of the men asked if he could have them for his tea. We found more in the engine compartment, above the exhaust manifold. If we'd driven off with them, it would have stunk the car out. What a dirty trick!

We drove off from the cheering dockers, and headed for Versailles. We had a meal and set off for Paris. We'd booked a hotel just off the Champs Elysees called … the Hotel Reynolds! It was in the same block as the famous Lido where they had all the glamorous shows. We booked ourselves a ticket, and they gave us a ringside chair and half a bottle of champagne. We had a great time.

After that we headed down through France and into Switzerland. In Geneva we were in a bar where people were dancing and a woman doing the paso doble ended up in my lap. Doreen wasn't impressed! We drove over St Bernard's Pass into the mountains, where we ate in a posh restaurant. I remember being amazed to see a poached egg on toast floating in my soup! We spent a night in Genoa, then Monaco. I hurt myself there when I dived off a forty-foot board into the swimming pool. I plunged so far down into the pool that the pressure hurt my ears, and I had to go to the doctor to get them fixed. He gave me some oil to drop into them. In the evening we went to lose some money in the casino. We went to Nice, then back to Paris via Grenoble. It was a very long trip, bearing in mind this was the early fifties and the roads weren't always great. The car went really well though, and I even managed to get involved in a rally which was going on. I raced as hard as I could against them even though I wasn't really entered. I couldn't resist it! I did my own navigation too, with just a map and compass.

As the years went by we went back to Paris quite often, and always got a mechanic friend to tune the car up before we left. On one occasion we'd just come onto the big junction at the Place de la Concorde. Cars come in from all over the place there, and I wanted to turn right. But there was a big taxi in the way, and the driver wasn't going to move over for me. So I just eased my car in front of him, just as if I was racing, and pushed him over. He ended up on the pavement. After all the years of competition, I wasn't going to let him get away with it!

We made our home at a flat in Springfield. Two years later I became a father when Christopher arrived. I was working on my racing car when I had an urgent phone call from Doctor Labesse: 'Come home quickly!' He was quite a character. I remember him sharing out gulps from his flask of whisky to the drivers at the line of the hill climb. 'Take some of that, you'll need it!' Anyway, I got home as fast as I could. The doctor told me that Doreen had been driving the car in the morning when someone had walked out in front of her. She'd braked hard, and the force had broken her waters, quite early. We wanted to take her to the maternity hospital, but she didn't want to go. So I got out the bottle of rum I had in the flat, and the two of us just sat there watching her. Eventually, at about eleven that night, she said, 'Yes, I had better go.' The doctor took her in my car and I drove his. In those days men didn't stay with their wives, so I didn't see Christopher being born.

A few years later Jacquie arrived, followed by Nicola soon afterwards.

But as one chapter in my life began, another ended. I was still spending a lot of time and money on racing cars, which were still a very important part of my life. I was even asked to race at international standard, which would have meant a huge amount of dedication. Bill Knight and Arthur Owens were racing Coopers and setting performance records, and they asked me to drive with them.

But it cost a lot to keep a racing car on the road, and with a young family to support I was finding it very hard. We had a new house which needed to be done up, and I just couldn't justify spending more time away from my wife and children. I had to work as well! I sold my car in 1955 and bought a cheaper one. That was a works MG, which looked like a Maserati, the one which I raffled to buy the go-kart. I had to be speeding around some kind of track, racing was in my veins, and I couldn't just let it go. But karting wasn't as fast or as much fun as racing my old Special, and eventually I agreed with Doreen that the time had come to be a bit more sensible. It was a huge wrench to stop racing, to lose that exhilarating feeling of speed and control I had found all the way through driving staff cars and ammo trucks, to hill climbs and sand races.

I took up golf, but that wasn't enough.

So I bought a boat. She was a thirty-three-foot twin-screw cabin cruiser, and I spent a whole year redesigning the interior. I turned it into a six-berth space, and made the wooden dashboard myself. It looked like new in the end, the mahogany shone in the sun, and I was really proud of her. It gave me a lot of satisfaction, and helped me to concentrate my mind on something other than cars.

The navigation skills which I had learned in the army came in useful too. On our first voyage we decided to sail to Granville in France, which is about fifteen miles east of Jersey. My best friend Al Gilbert was with us, and he enjoyed a drink or two. He was meant to be on the wheel while the rest of us went downstairs and played poker. But he put this novice chap in control instead, so he could relax. Anyway, at about nine o'clock I thought we should have been ready to go into port at Granville. So I went up the ladder and looked around, and couldn't see anything at all except for three lights in the distance. I checked the charts, and they told me that it was Granville – but a long way off! I went to the wheel myself, and was lucky to take us in on the high tide because I didn't have a clue about all the rocks around there. It was probably the first time in my life that I was lucky on a boat!

Once we learned our way about, we went all over the place from our base in Jersey. Up to eight of us could sleep in her, from the wheelhouse to the small space in the back cabin.

I did have some other luck with boats years later. The Bouley Bay Boat Owners Club had a dinner with a special draw, with tickets at fifty pounds each. You could win a car and speedboat. I asked for ticket number ninety-two, but it was already taken. I had to settle for number ninety-one. Most people on our table had tickets in the nineties, and when the first digit drawn out of the hat was nine, we all got really excited. My friend Ray had managed to get the ticket I wanted – ninety-two – but the next number drawn out was one! 'Serves you bloody right!' I said to Ray. I didn't need a boat or another car though, so they gave us a cash prize instead. We spent the money on our first ever flying holiday when we went to Mallorca.

Many years later cars came back into my life, but it was my son Christopher who brought it about. He had seen pictures of me racing, and watched other people doing it, and he told me he wanted to be a racing driver himself. I warned him off it though, because the sport had cost me so much time and money. I invited him to join me in the business, but he decided to become a ship's engineer. He was in the Merchant Navy, then worked for Shell on their big tankers, then on cargo boats taking wheat to Japan.

Because he was away at sea for so long in his job he saved lots of money, and every time he came back from a long voyage he'd spend it all on a vintage car. In 1972 he bought a beautiful 1932 Lagonda, which I still have in my garage. But it took me a while to appreciate what he had. When he first brought it home, I said, 'Why on earth have you spent money on an old thing like that?' Because in my day, we used to take old cars, strip them down and race them over the sand until they fell to bits. The war was over, and everyone wanted new things. They didn't want to look backwards, but forwards. The higher and more recent your car's registration number, the better. I didn't realise that the old ones were becoming increasingly valuable. We've had it restored since, which cost thousands of pounds. Twenty years ago we were offered a hundred thousand pounds for it. I even bought an original low number plate for it.

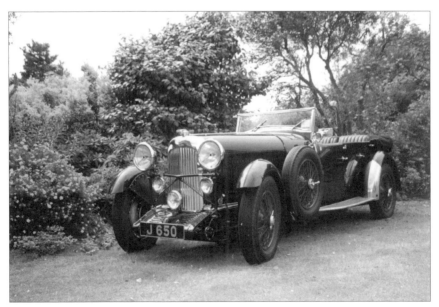

The 1932 Lagonda

145

In my eighties and still racing in the Lagonda in a Jersey hill climb

When I saw how enthusiastic Christopher was, I started to take a real interest in the cars he was finding. I drove a four and a half litre M-45 Lagonda, which was quite rare, an E-Type Jaguar, and a beautiful old 1921 Sunbeam Tourer among others.

The one in the garage is my favourite. She's a lovely racing green, with a great-sounding engine. I keep her clean and polished and always ready for a spin.

I've taken her away on holiday many times, often to shows and rallies on the Continent. Although they aren't really races, they can still be quite competitive. Sometimes they would have driving test competitions, to see how well you could handle the cars. I won the test one year at Deauville, when I was seventy-five. I beat about a hundred other people.

Taking the old cars away and showing them off gives me as much pleasure as racing used to. They look so much better, with so much more class, than modern cars. Of course they aren't perfect, they leak oil every now and again, but that's part of their charm. Modern cars all look the same, and never really go wrong. Where's the excitement in that?

I suppose I've slowed down a bit recently; I'm in my nineties now, and a bit more nervous. But when I get onto a motorway I'll still put my foot down and enjoy the speed of it. I consider myself a fair driver still, and often moan about older people driving too slowly and getting in my way!

CHAPTER 14

TIME TO TELL MY STORY

When the war ended and I came home, I tried to forget all about it. I didn't want to remember all the terrible things I had seen. I threw myself into the racing, into my work, and into family life. I didn't talk about the war to anyone, no one asked me about it, and I was happy for my memories to fade away. I didn't discuss it with my brothers, and all I ever told Doreen was that I'd been a soldier. I joined lots of clubs, but there was a sort of agreement that we never talked about the war; it was like a band of friendship. I even lost touch with Willy Willmore, who I'd been so close to through all the dangers we'd faced together. Every year the *News of the World* used to publish details of reunions for army units, but I never went to them. They were always held in London, and I never had enough time to go over there.

I had nightmares sometimes, especially about German planes. I would re-live the bombings in London, in Liverpool and in Holland, where I'd seen so many people killed and so much destruction. I would wake up frightened, because they had reminded me of dreadful things. We never had the psychological help they offer servicemen these days, and they weren't so good at dealing with what we now call post-traumatic stress. I can remember one man in our unit being court-martialled because he had been so scared of going into battle that he'd shot his own toe off. They had no understanding of the fear and pressure we were under.

I did go and watch the war films which came out, especially in the fifties and sixties when they tried to tell the story of what we had done. I didn't always like them though. I saw *A Bridge Too Far*, the story of Operation Market Garden, and it seemed to be all about the Americans. Our contribution was hardly mentioned. The sounds of shooting and explosions in the films often brought the war back to me, but it was nice to feel secure in a cinema instead of hiding in my foxhole! To me, the best war films are the ones which don't dwell on the guns and bombs, but the ones which look at the feelings and emotions of the men who are fighting.

Eventually, I managed to blank a lot of my past out. The war became a distant memory, and the things I had seen and done faded away, just as I hoped they would. I worked hard, raised my family, and travelled the world on some wonderful holidays. I think I've visited most countries in the world apart from Russia and New Zealand. I've cruised on the Yangtze River, and been on safari in Africa.

But on the fiftieth anniversary of the liberation of Jersey, things changed. It was 9 May, 1995, and the island was holding an even bigger celebration than usual. I was in the Lagonda at a vintage car rally at the People's Park in town. A man came up to me and told me how much he loved the car, and we chatted about it for a while. But I noticed he had some medals on his chest, and I asked him why. 'We've just formed a Normandy Veterans Association.' he said. I told him I'd been in Normandy too, and he said I should join them. So I joined, even though I didn't have any medals. I'd never asked for any, and they'd never sent me any. After talking to some of the other veterans, I sent away for the ones I was eligible for, and was quite proud to get them. I was one short though, the Defence Medal, and I ended up buying my own. I even found an old Royal Army Service Corps cap badge in a shop in England, which I bought to fix to my new blue beret.

Once I'd joined the group, I started to talk about the war again. One chap who I had a lot in common with was Clive Kemp, who'd been a sapper building bridges for the tanks and soldiers to cross rivers. We'd been in a lot of the same places and actions, for example Falaise, the push into Belgium and Market Garden. We remembered a lot of the same things, despite all the years. It really was like meeting an old comrade.

It's funny how things come back. When we went to events we often had to march behind a band, and we could all remember how to do it. We'd stride out, swinging our arms, maybe not quite as fast as we used to but we did quite well.

Me second from the right with some of the Normandy veterans,
Sword Beach (Courtesy Jersey Evening Post)

The first time I went back to Normandy was with some friends in a minibus. We decided it would be interesting to see the beaches and battlefields, so we took a short trip there. I remembered Bayeux in particular, because we'd been in a field nearby for a while. It was also where I had been arrested by the Military Police, so not all the memories were happy ones! We drove through Caen too, and saw how they had repaired it after it had been so shattered during the fighting.

Then the sixtieth anniversary of D-Day came along, and a whole load of us from Jersey went across to join the commemorations. The Queen was going to be there, with lots of world leaders and politicians. We were on a big coach, along with hundreds of others. Unfortunately, the organisation was a real shambles because of security concerns, and we spent a lot of time sitting around waiting.

But there were some lovely times. Everywhere we went the people welcomed us, clapping and cheering, and we were given medals from the people of Normandy.

We marched through a village, with all the children waving and cheering. They had special T-shirts on, thanking veterans for what they had done. We were in a parade with lots of other veterans and modern soldiers. I felt so proud to be part of that, and the sergeant major in charge said our turnout and marching had been wonderful.

The seventieth anniversary was quite different. A lot of our veterans had died, or couldn't come, and so myself and Harry Fenn went over together. Harry had served in the Navy, and had ferried supplies on and off the beaches. We went with the photographer Tony Pike, and had a fantastic time. From the moment we got on the ferry from Jersey we were really honoured by so many people. The captain invited us to the bridge and showed us around, and the other passengers wanted to know all about us.

In the morning of 6 June, we left our hotel in Avranches to go towards Bayeux. We had to leave really early because they were expecting traffic jams. But when we got to Caen, it was already completely gridlocked, with road blocks and barriers everywhere. They were expecting all sorts of important people, and security was really tight.

Then all of a sudden we were surrounded by police motorcycles. The riders recognised that we were veterans trying to get to the memorial service. They set off, sirens wailing, to clear a path for us! When we got into the centre, we got onto a coach which had some other veterans and friends on it. The police motorcyclists stayed with us, three at the front and two at the back, and drove us right through the centre of town. We went through all the red lights, all the barriers, all the stop signs, as they stopped the traffic for us. We felt like really important people ourselves! I don't think the Queen could have been treated better.

When we got to the cemetery in Bayeux where the service was going to happen, Tony grabbed some front row seats for us. We were very close to the Queen and the other dignitaries, and we were even seen on the BBC television coverage of the event. When it finished, Tony pushed us to make sure we were presented to all the dignitaries. We met Prince Charles first. He came down the line of veterans, and they all looked very serious when they spoke to him. I thought I might be able to cheer him up. When he got down to me, he said 'Oh, you come from Jersey. I suppose you must have been able to speak French to the people when you arrived in 1944?' 'Well Sir, not really,' I said. 'Only some schoolboy phrases and things. But I did learn enough to say to a young lady, "*Voulez-vous coucher avec moi ce soir?*"' And he laughed his head off. 'And what about the Calvados?' he asked me. I told him the Calvados had come in very handy when we had been hiding in ditches to get away from the bombs and shells they were throwing at us!

We also said hello to Camilla, and lots of politicians like David Cameron and Ed Miliband. They all wanted to shake our hands and wish us well.

Then Tony drove us to Arromanches, and wanted to take pictures of us on the beach. Harry didn't want to go at first, but I encouraged him, and we ended up looking out to sea by the Mulberry Harbour where I had brought ammunition ashore seventy-one years before. The picture was in the *Jersey Evening Post*. A journalist from Reuters interviewed me, and the

'Voulez-vous coucher avec moi?' (*Courtesy Jersey Evening Post*)

Daily Telegraph interviewed Harry.

That wasn't my only brush with royalty either. Our Association was invited to send veterans to Buckingham Palace, through the Not Forgotten Club. Hundreds were invited from across the country, for a tea party. We dressed up carefully, with all our medals polished up. At the correct time we went in through a side entrance, through a huge courtyard, and into the gardens at the back of the Palace. There were all sorts of people there, not just veterans. I saw Esther Rantzen and other celebrities all chatting to each other. We enjoyed our tea and met lots of people. I spoke to Prince Edward, who asked me what I had done during the war. I told him all about my service in Normandy and Germany. Seventy years ago, I was just one of thousands of ordinary soldiers, just doing my job. I never would have dreamed that one day I would be invited to Buckingham Palace for tea!

In recent years, people in Jersey have taken much more interest in who we are and what we did. We always seem to be in the paper, and people

Harry, the Mulberry Harbour and me at Arromanches
(*Courtesy Jersey Evening Post*)

stop me and ask me about my story. We had a lot of publicity after the seventieth anniversary in particular. I think it's great, and I believe that the new generations should hear about what we did. After all the years of keeping quiet, and no one wanting to know, I enjoy telling everyone about it.

People often ask me how I feel about Germans today. I realised even while the war was still going on that lots of German people didn't actually want the war. They wanted to live normal lives, and didn't have any hatred for anyone. But of course there were the Nazis, the ones who had been brainwashed by Hitler and his cronies, and they were the worst sort – the ones who persecuted the Jews, who murdered and tortured people. I never had any sympathy with them, and I don't now.

There were hundreds of Jersey boys who served in the war. Not just in Normandy, but also in the Far East, in the air force, and in the navy and Atlantic convoys. We've had medals and recognition from so many French councils and organisations; and just this year the Normandy veterans were presented with badges from the people of Jersey. Without the sacrifice that so many Jersey men made, the island would still be under the Germans, after all.

Life in the army was good for me. When I look back, I think I enjoyed the opportunities it gave me. I learned to strip and rebuild an engine, to drive all sorts of vehicles, and to have confidence in myself. I learned to iron my clothes and how to repair my socks. Above all I learned discipline, which was very good for me.

When we march or go on parade now, people clap and cheer us. It's a wonderful feeling, and I feel great that I was there, and that I did all these things that people read about in history books. It's lovely that they appreciate it. I am proud to be a veteran, and proud that I did my bit.

Chris Stone is a broadcaster and writer with a particular interest in the wartime exploits of the soldiers, sailors and airmen who, very modestly, 'did their bit' in the last war.

He has worked for the BBC in Jersey for more than twenty years, and feels privileged to have interviewed many of the brave men, and women, who put their lives at risk because their country, and their island, needed them to.

He is proud to call some of them friends.